Ivy Compton-Burnett

Ivy Compton-Burnett

Barbara Hardy

EDINBURGH
University Press

Edinburgh University Press is one of the leading university presses in the UK. We publish academic books and journals in our selected subject areas across the humanities and social sciences, combining cutting-edge scholarship with high editorial and production values to produce academic works of lasting importance.
For more information visit our website:
www.edinburghuniversitypress.com

Edinburgh University Press Ltd
The Tun – Holyrood Road
12 (2f) Jackson's Entry
Edinburgh EH8 8PJ

Typeset in 10.5 on 13 Sabon by
Iolaire Typesetting, Newtonmore and
printed and bound in Great Britain by
CPI Group (UK) Ltd, Croydon CR0 4YY

A CIP record for this book is available from the British Library

ISBN 978 1 4744 0134 0 (hardback)
ISBN 978 1 4744 0136 4 (webready PDF)
ISBN 978 1 4744 0135 7 (paperback)
ISBN 978 1 4744 0137 1 (epub)

Contents

Acknowledgements

I am grateful to Ernest, Julia and Kate Hardy for sharing my enjoyment of Ivy Compton-Burnett, to Maud Ellmann for proposing I should write this book, and for her help, to my friends Isobel Armstrong, Martin Dodsworth, Janet El-Rayess, Miranda El-Rayess, Loraine Fletcher, Graham Handley, Tom Healy and Sue Roe, for comment and argument, to Martha Thompson for library work, to Patrick Davies for indispensable research assistance of many kinds, and to the libraries of the University of London, and Kensington and Chelsea.

The Publisher and Series Editor regret to say that Barbara died shortly after she had given final approval for the proofs and sadly did not live to see the printed volume published.

Series Editor's Preface
Midcentury Modern Writers

Midcentury Modern Writers opens new vistas in modernist studies by restoring undervalued writers, genres, and literary movements to the twentieth-century literary canon. The reasons for this critical neglect are manifold, but they include a tenacious bias in favour of male writers associated with the European metropolis, especially London and Paris. Even Virginia Woolf was begrudged a place in the pantheon of 'High Modernism' until the resurgence of feminism in the 1970s. Meanwhile, other distinguished women writers of the midcentury, along with their male contemporaries, have receded from view, overshadowed by towering figures like Joyce and Eliot.

The purpose of this series is not to topple these figures but to enrich our sense of the contestation between forms and genres in the midcentury period, roughly from 1928 (when British women were finally granted the vote on equal terms with men) to the 1960s. The traditional modernist canon, comprising a small band of experimental pioneers, obscures not only the creative wealth and variety of these five decades but even those features that distinguish modernists from their literary rivals. A fresh view of the period, undistorted by the fetishisation of modernism, reveals that the mainstream is often difficult to distinguish from its tributaries; tradition and experiment overlap in ways that disrupt conventional critical taxonomies and hierarchies. Likewise, highbrow and popular literary forms galvanise each other, despite the so-called 'great divide' that critics have imposed between them.

Midcentury Modern Writers includes both single-author studies and wide-ranging thematic and generic surveys of the period. The authors of these original studies have been selected from established and emergent voices in Anglophone literary studies on the basis of their expertise, inventiveness, and clarity, in the expectation that this series will open up new avenues of investigation for students and their teachers, as well as for specialists in the field. Ultimately, this series strives to change the way we read, teach, and study modern writing in English.

General Editor
Maud Ellmann

To my daughters
Julia and Kate Hardy
with love

Introduction

Compton-Burnett is one of the most original twentieth-century writers, modernist in art, and in social attitude superficially conservative but implicitly subversive in several ways. Most of her novels, like those of Dickens and George Eliot, gain perspective by being set in the England of her childhood and adolescence.[1] Born in Pinner into a middle-class family in 1884, her father a homeopathic doctor and speculative builder, she wrote about the landed gentry, later giving friends the impression that this was her background.[2] Her mother, Katherine Rees, was Thomas Compton Burnett's second wife: a bad stepmother, prototype for her daughter's domestic tyrants, and a snob who added the hyphen to their name. Ivy's elder brother, Guy, died of pneumonia in 1905, her two youngest sisters committed suicide together in 1917, her younger brother, Noel, was killed at the Battle of the Somme in 1917, his young widow attempted suicide, and Ivy nearly died in the post-war influenza epidemic. She had taken her turn as household oppressor till her younger sisters left home for musical careers, sharing house with the pianist, Myra Hess, and declining to have their elder sister to stay. However, she managed family properties and investments, and when she died in 1969, her surviving sisters were generous with biographical information. The love of her life was the antique-furniture expert, Margaret Jourdain, with whom she lived in sexless harmony and creative discord from 1919 until Margaret died in 1951, leaving Ivy inconsolable in their Cornwall Gardens flat (south-west London, round the corner from T. S. Eliot) but supported by friends.

Widely read in fiction from Jane Austen to Iris Murdoch, she thought Virginia Woolf over-rated and was jealous of better-sellers like Rose Macaulay and Daphne du Maurier. Her novels, published between 1911 and 1971, were adapted for radio, stage and television, and she was admired by brilliant reviewers like Elizabeth Bowen and Edward

Sackville-West, and praised by Mario Praz and *nouvelle vague* Nathalie Sarraute. She gave the impression that she was hard-up but was turned down for a – second – Royal Literary Fund grant after her large private income was disclosed. She was given the James Tait Black prize, an honorary doctorate from Leeds, a CBE and a DBE. She hankered after better sales with bigger royalties, and relations with her long-term publisher, Victor Gollancz, were not harmonious. Her high-life novels seem to be odd fellows for his Left Book Club series, but there may be a kinship: narrowly and complacently conservative in social views and assumptions, she is revolutionary in language, reflexive form and some deep insights.[3]

She was educated by tutors and governesses, a school in Hove for 'the Daughters of Gentlemen', and London University's Royal Holloway College, where she took an Upper-Second in classics, reading Plato and the Greek dramatists who helped to shape her philosophy and form. Innovative and reflexive like James Joyce and T. S. Eliot, but never a critic or theorist with a manifesto, she cuts moral appeal, long description and stage direction. Like her contemporary, Henry Green, she re-invents Thomas Love Peacock's taut conversation-novel and Henry James's dramatically shaped narrative. She disliked symbolist novels but *Darkness and Day* uses imagistic form. She requires time, concentration and effort, challenging moralities, enlarging experience and exciting imagination.

Her philosophical link is with post-Darwinian agnosticism, though not for her the humanist ethic and symbolism rooted in Christianity, which Eliot got from Feuerbach. She is strongly rationalist. Her unwritten credo is Brecht's: she urges reason, not tragic catharsis or empathy, and her cool, amused spectators are like his detached analytic *raisonneurs*, commentators who distance us from sympathy and admiration to make us face the problems of being human. Like Brecht, she is not always consistent, and as we admire and pity his Mother Courage, we may admire and pity her truth-tellers. She was a modernist unawares, and anticipates postmodernists in asserting reflexivity and denying us soft, readerly pleasures of moral assent and optimistic identification. Her novels are difficult emotionally as well as intellectually because they rebuke what Ortega y Gasset calls 'sentimental intervention'.[4]

Themes are explicit or implicit in the playful titles which draw attention to language as medium and theme. In scrutinising the language of thought processes, she is like linguistic philosophers but less abstract. In foregrounding language, she is like postmodernist language poets but more accessible. Like all good narrative artists, she intuitively analyses narrative imagination, telling stories within stories, concentrating on the secrets, lies and gossip which corrupt candour.

Like Thackeray, she wants to make readers uncomfortable, using comedy to face mortal discomforts and refusing to exalt humanity, but she is more austere, making us reason and reflect – or put the book down. Novelists will go on inviting us to identify and sympathise, but the genre has been enlarged by her demands, and after reading her we should read every book more thoughtfully. Now and then, she shows and arouses strong feeling, complexly and quietly: in *A God and His Gifts*, a mother watches a child who does not know she is his mother; in *Manservant and Maidservant*, a girl's eyes fill with tears as she hears a kind word; in *Darkness and Day*, a fat, middle-aged woman looks at a photograph of herself when young and desirable; and in *A House and Its Head*, a delirious, dying mother asks her plain, clumsy daughter if she is the beautiful girl-child of her dreams. We are enlightened by such movements of feeling, and dwell on them because we cannot pin them down and give them a name.[5]

Her feminist themes[6] are implicit in the drama of bad marriages, suffering wives and dutiful daughters, explicated by sharp-sighted sceptical observers: Emily Herrick says it is terrible to do your duty, knows why she and William Masson will never marry, and props up her self-deceiving brother; her confidante, Theresa Fletcher, resents bearing sons to be killed (*Pastors and Masters*); and Hope Cranmer (*Parents and Children*) and Rachel Hardisty (*Men and Wives*) are second wives amused by predecessors, husbands and step-children, Hope casting a cold eye on her friend's mothering, Rachel helping neurotic Harriet and her family. Undemonstrative Gretchen Jekyll is loved by her boy-pupils, spots murder, reviles scandal, and on her deathbed tells a hard truth about loving daughter more than son. These cool realists comment drily, know what they are doing, see the funny side of life and see life whole. They perceive the power of nurture and question myths of nature: mothers do not find that mothering comes naturally, children love nurse best. Compton-Burnett has no use for conventions of gender role. Sexual preference and habit are changed without fuss, in variation not deviation. A man sits on another man's knee, as matter of fact. One or two are mildly teased for a camp style: Julian Wake jokes about his vase of columbines (*Brothers and Sisters*), Elton Scrope about his careful tea-making (*The Present and the Past*) but the fun is made by, not at, such self-styled, 'womanly' men. Many wise women and men are happily unmarried. Sibling love often brings deep content, once or twice when it is incestuous. Incest, actual or imaginary, is a subject which does not rise here to the argumentative or analytic status of theme, but like adultery and excessive parental or filial attachment, it is presented coolly, even teasingly. Unshocked, the novelist dares us to be unshocked also, to take or leave such aspects of human life. Her treatment of incest also reflects on the classical drama she never re-read but never forgot.

She makes explicit and internalises an awareness of environment. An unswerving conservative who blamed Labour for social ills even when Tories were in power, she shows conscious and unconscious insight into class, family, wealth and property. Power is dramatised in domestic oppressions which had a personal origin, but she recognised their larger relevance: for instance, to the politics 'of divine right and the acceptance of it'.[7] More deeply and originally, she sees the creature in its circumstance, and mediates contingency and conditioning through her individual characters. This is the theme that led her, no doubt unconsciously, to write about the landed gentry; only an estate and a heritage could act as a sufficient metonymy.

Her other large social theme is dramatised and described but never conceptualised: it is domestic culture, displayed in everyday routines and pastimes. She saw plot as essential to structure but records the passage of daily life closely and circumstantially; her plots turn on sensational events like adultery, illegitimacy, bigamy, incest and murder but, like Chekhov, whom she admired, she sets them in the flow of ordinary happenings, and whatever else her people do, they go on eating, drinking, joking, playing, writing and reading. These things are the surfaces and the stuff of life, and she implies rather than explicates their deep significances.

After discussing these aspects of her art and themes, I end with readings of *Elders and Betters* and *Darkness and Day*. The first brings us close to a disturbingly unsympathetic figure; the other distances a sympathetic one. Her demanding and amusing novels are alive to the pleasures, pains and passions of life, consciously and unconsciously trying to tell truths about human beings.

Notes

1. 'I do not feel that I have any real or organic knowledge of life later than about 1910' (Margaret Jourdain and Ivy Compton-Burnett, 'A Conversation between I. Compton-Burnett and Margaret Jourdain', in *The Art of I. Compton-Burnett*, ed. Burkhart, 27). For all publication details see the Bibliography.

2. Unless otherwise stated, biographical information is from Hilary Spurling's *Ivy When Young* and *Secrets of a Woman's Heart*.
3. But see Alison Light's reading of the novelist's conservatism in *Forever England*.
4. Ortega y Gasset, *The Dehumanization of Art*, 9.
5. I disagree with Light's judgement that 'emotional temperature varies very little from novel to novel: it is always chilly' (*Forever England*, 21).
6. Compton-Burnett's feminism is discussed by Kathy Justice Gentile, *Ivy Compton-Burnett*.
7. Jourdain and Compton-Burnett, 'A Conversation', in *The Art of I. Compton-Burnett*, ed. Burkhart, 29.

Chapter 1

The Title and Its Text

Coleridge praised *The Winter's Tale* as 'exquisitely respondent to its title'[1] and this is true of many Compton-Burnett novels. Other novelists have used subtle, suggestive and poetic titles but I do not think anybody else has written eighteen titles[2] in the same artful form.

Finding a title for your book is like and also unlike naming your child. The child's name is usually given soon after its birth but whenever the book's name is chosen by the author, its full meaning is deferred, developed and not confirmed until the conclusion – or afterthought. Ideally, the book should be matched by its name, which should sum it up not too simply, alert and attract readers not too blatantly, and promote tension, expectation and surprise. Compton-Burnett's witty and dynamic titles fulfil these functions, and though their similarity may make the range look narrow, it is wide.

As Coleridge praises *The Winter's Tale*'s title, he teases us into the thought, 'But isn't it the other way round? Surely the title responds to the play?' Invited by a great writer's wit, we contemplate the play's surface, depth, characters, images, themes, pattern, ending, and the complex act of naming a work of art. Compton-Burnett's titles are provocative in asserting their common subject of social and biological kinship and their own semantic and poetic kinship. The titles work singly and as a series which compounds form and rhetoric, accumulating sense, making a joke that gets funnier but is never simply funny, each time it is repeated making us think 'What, another one of these titles?' till we reach the posthumous *The Last and the First*, and a last laugh. The novels are about the family, and their titles form a family.

Pastors and Masters rhymes. *The Last and the First* half-rhymes. Nine titles alliterate, like *A Family and a Fortune*; three assonate, like *Elders and Betters*; some are antithetical, like *The Present and the Past*; nine are parallels, like *Pastors and Masters*; some echo and question common-place phrases, like *Pastors and Masters* and *Elders and Betters*; eleven refer specifically to family relations, and the rest to abstractions which the novels particularise and demonstrate in family relations. *Elders and Betters* is a hendiadys.[3] The balance, parallelism or opposition in the titles after *Dolores* (1911) invite readers to contemplate their kind, function and relationship. The exception, *Bullivant and the Lambs*, the title of the American edition of *Manservant and Maidservant*, was changed at Knopf's wish, and deviates from the original title by opposing classes and using proper names. Compton-Burnett raised no objection, longing for more fame and money, and casual about changes such as those made in radio and theatre versions of her books. The English title may suggest a story about gender but the novel is more concerned with abuses of power, though we come to see that the title signals a concern with class.

Naming a book is not quite the same as naming a painting or a symphony, which requires the painter and the composer to move outside their medium, and less is expected of their word-making – by themselves or others. It may be best to be modestly obvious, and call the work 'Portrait of a Young Man'. (In *Darkness and Day*, a playful grandmother, Selina, invents this sort of title for imaginary portraits depicting herself and her sons.) The painting is often given a title because its subject seems obvious, but apart from programmatic works, music is less well served: the composer may simply give opus, key and instrument references. Words describing music – unless it is music with words – are not obligatory and are often conferred by other people. The title of a book is an essential and prominent part of the writer's art and enterprise, expected by publishers, separate from text but not from book, on the cover, the spine, the title page, at the head of every page or every other page if there are alternate running heads, a beginning but also an ending since we read it again and read it differently as and after we finish the story.

Many novelists agonise over errors and trials of choice. Dickens thought of calling his eighth novel *Nobody's Fault* but this would have been too pat a summing-up of one theme, too little concerned with a heroine close to her author in creative love. Little Dorrit's imagination is at the heart of the novel, and her author uses the name bestowed by Arthur Clennam, friend and lover; we read his affectionate naming in the light of the title, read the title differently after it, and again at the end when author's and character's namings can come together in full strength. George Eliot thought of *Sister Maggie*, too directed towards one character, then of *The Tullivers*, too directed to the group, so when her publisher suggested *The Mill on the Floss*, she sacrificed precision (the mill was not on the Floss but on its tributary) for a synecdochic image of women and men in their environment, her deep subject.

When Samuel Richardson called his first novel *Pamela*, he kept the reader guessing – would the virtuous but savvy heroine stay single? When he called his second novel *Clarissa Harlowe*, he was hinting that the heroine would never marry, though readers might not take it in till her long agony was over. But when Theodor Fontane called his novel *Effi Briest*, he was not revealing the outcome for Effi but doing the opposite, since she marries and changes her maiden name. All the same, her author, like Clarissa's, knew what he was doing, anticipating Effi's – and the book's – final critique of her marriage and the social pressures that make marriages, and his title reflects his deep theme. Compton-Burnett knew what she was doing, as she continued and flaunted her clever elegant titles.

She admired Jane Austen and Elizabeth Gaskell, and *Sense and Sensibility*, *Pride and Prejudice* and *Wives and Daughters* may have suggested her carefully and teasingly mutated titles. (*Wives and Daughters* is also interesting because Edward Sackville-West noticed that its dialogue, compared by one listening character to strophe and antistrophe in Greek drama, anticipated Compton-Burnett's.)[4] The novel compares many wives and daughters, dwelling on Mrs Hadley, Mrs Gibson, Molly and Cynthia, and the title points to the moral, psychological and social implications of a pattern. So did Stendhal's *Le Rouge et le Noir*, Tolstoy's *War and Peace*, Carlyle's *Past and Present*, Turgenev's *Fathers and Sons* and D. H. Lawrence's *Sons and Lovers*. It was a familiar form which Compton-Burnett adopted and made strange.

All her novels are about power and possessions, observed in family life and metonymised by family life, but an accompanying preoccupation of those written after the 1914–18 war is language, in which we speak, think, write and read. After writing *Dolores*, which followed Richardson, Charlotte Smith, Fanny Burney, Fontane and many others by using a heroine's name for its title, Compton-Burnett wrote the other books where most titles underline the family theme but are also made linguistically assertive by grammar, balance and rhythm. The structure of each title, emphasised individually and recurring to make a species, links two nouns or substantive adjectives, usually in parallel or antithesis. The double substantive chimes with Compton-Burnett's concentration on dialogic form, and the titles' patterns reflect, and reflect on, her constant, profound and reflexive concern with the arts of language.

I do not suggest that the title of *Pastors and Masters* (1925) was designed with all these characteristics in mind. Some titles are more complex or ironic than others and their relation to their novel varies. Compton-Burnett acknowledged the unconscious element in imagination[5] and may not have grown conscious of the art of titles until she wrote the second or third novel in her new distinctive style. Nor, of course, would she have been conscious of all the allusions to the title within the novel. The title *Pastors and Masters* has rhyme, balance and parallelism, and is a common phrase used simple-mindedly or ironically. She uses it literally and on occasion metaphorically: she has two feeble Church of England vicars, a tyrannical father who has been a clergyman, a do-gooder who has an evening class for her 'dear men things', and several school-teachers, male and female, bad and good, qualified and unqualified. Not one is a good pastor or master of anything, though the egregious Mr Merry, satisfyingly called 'a nincompoop' long after we have seen that this is what he is, has mastered the art of soft-soaping present and prospective parents, his employer and the maid. There are three academic masters: Nicholas Herrick, the Head and owner of a school, and graduate of the Oxbridge-like local university, does no work except for saying morning prayers, networking on speech day, and having a shot at literary plagiarism; Richard Bumpus and William Masson are old friends and fellows of an unnamed college in the unnamed university. Everyone is a pastor or master or both, except the schoolboys, and the rational, articulate and imaginative women at the heart of the novel, Emily Herrick and Griselda Fletcher. They are feminist versions of Berthold Brecht's depersonalising and analytic *raisonneur*, and Emily's fond, amused tolerance of her weak brother is masterly and pastoral. All but one of the professional pastors and masters – Masson – is self-serving, dishonest, idle and incompetent, though usually not unlikeable; their author had a soft spot for all her characters.[6] The traditional and familiar words of the title belong only to the author, the coupling never appearing in the text, where masters are called school-master, under-master, teacher and educationist, and clergy called clergyman, parson and chaplain. The accumulation of pastors and masters is a joke in itself.

The title *Brothers and Sisters* (1929), often repeated in the text, has a clear application, though the family subject grows an extra meaning when marital relationships turn out to be incestuous, and more when the action reveals new surprising aspects, as these novels often do after we think the revelations are over. The six brother-and-sister pairs make a cumulative and reflexive joke, like the innumerable pastors and masters, the repeated phrase making sure we readers do not miss it. This is done by elaboration:

> 'Here is a dear party of brothers and sisters. Because that is what you must be, isn't it? We know that Gilbert and Caroline are a funny pair of brother and sister to Father really. But that is not what we want. So we will have you all brothers and sisters together.' (90)[7]

It is done by repetition: 'The Drydens were a pale, tall brother and sister' (44) and 'Sarah and Julian Wake were another brother and sister' (45) and '"That is another brother and sister we shall be," said Tilly, in a dubious tone' (47) and Tilly's 'we shall not be all brothers and sisters together here much longer,' followed by her father's 'Not brothers and sisters!' (66). And it is done by innuendo: Julian says with a knowing inflection, 'the engagement of more brothers and sisters would be best glossed over' (218) and Peter says, 'here is a beautiful group of boys and girls, of brothers and sisters – and everything!' (219). But the brother-and-sister theme is not the only one, and the repeated title presides rather lightly over the novel; the affective centre and depth of the action is a mother's emotional oppression of her children, though it is suggested that this springs from her especially intense and close relationship with her husband–brother.

More Women than Men (1933) has a title with more than one interpretation, but the question of gender is there from the start, as the novel opens in the setting of a girls' school, with a company of women who dominate the action as social majority and centre of interest. There are a few men: the headmistress Josephine's husband, stolen from a friend; her nephew and adopted son, Gabriel, to whom she is for some time jealously devoted; her brother; and Felix Bacon, the music teacher. At the end, Josephine, who has a heterosexual history, and Maria Rosetti, one of her teachers, who seems to be bisexual, embrace each other for a collaboration in love and work. The male characters are faded out, except for Felix, who moves without drama from a long, contented homosexual relationship to a title, an inheritance and an attractive Oxford First-Class wife. Though some characters occasionally comment on their own sexuality, the sexual shifts are managed by characters and author without a fuss, quietness making its point, helped by that cunning title.

The scene moves two or three times to houses where the 'head' is male, but the school is ruled and almost entirely manned by women, and the response to the title seems clear and simple. However, Compton-Burnett makes it impossible for the active reader – and she makes her reader very active – to read words without scrutinising them closely. I wrote 'clear and simple' but as we follow mutating meanings, here and in most of her other novels, it becomes clear sooner or later – sometimes very soon, sometimes not till the end – that there is more to the title than the theme we first notice. After the first two or three books, the repeated title form, with its emphasis on language, persuades us to look hard at word and phrase, and ask more than obvious questions.

The title *More Women than Men* makes us ponder the effect of having more women than men. At the end, does it matter as much as it seems to at the beginning when the headmistress interviews her staff on their return from holiday, dramatising her own benevolent power and competence, when the single women are defensive or apologetic or evasive or jokey, accepting marriage as the desirable norm and spinsterdom the regrettable deviation, and when much is made of the new bright girl – who is quickly married off rather than given a career? Or when Josephine appoints a man to teach music and join the all-woman senior common room? Or when she assumes and dramatises a state of married bliss, and falsifies her relationships with her husband and her nephew, actions leading to two tragic deaths: one an accident which would not have happened without sexual rivalry, and one which is a *crime passionnel*? Or when the happy ending is the professional and sexual partnership of two strong women?

Though the book is set in Victorian middle-class society some time before the 1914–18 war, we may extend its title's prompting to the special relevance of the early 1920s, when there were more women than men because of war deaths. (Compton-Burnett's brother died in the Battle of the Somme.) In the novel and in the real world, past and present, women sometimes have to do without men, as Compton-Burnett's generation – though not the pre-war characters in this post-war novel – had to. And in all periods, women sometimes choose to do without men, and prefer to. The novel's title points the reader to these implications and expansions, though both particular and general meanings move together in conjunction or oscillation. Both title and story reflect the author's double historical vision, one of her gifts. She said she could only grasp her own Victorian past as whole and organic, but in fact she is remarkably alive to past and present.

A House and Its Head (1935) refreshes and makes us scrutinise literal and metonymic senses of 'House' and 'Head'. Some characters articulate these meanings: Duncan Edgeworth's second wife, Alison, astonished as the grown-up children rise to retire when their father says he is going to bed, asks, 'Do you always go to bed at the nod of the head of the house?' (129). The collocation of Head and House is important in text and title: Duncan's sense of being 'over' his family is repeated several times, in association with the sense of house as patriarchal possession and his proud pleasure in the son and heir his first oppressed wife has never 'given' him. This is also related to his misogyny and the preference for male company he shares with other men in the novels. Compton-Burnett's feminism is demonstrated indirectly, not argued explicitly, and this novel's title is very slowly revealed as criticising male prerogatives.

The ever-present House is stripped of specification, suspended in time and space, stranger and more abstract because we know nothing about its place, site, size, appearance, furniture, grounds, architecture or period. The absence of physical particularity is important and makes itself felt. It is sometimes said that all Compton-Burnett's post-war novels are set at the end of the nineteenth century, with anachronisms – for instance, divorce law and transport – but in *A House and Its Head* the characters mention 'Victorian' mores, plainly indicating a later period, though the historical vagueness helps to isolate and conceptualise the subject announced in title and subtly responsive text.

Duncan asks his daughter aggressively, 'And are you the head of the house, or am I?' and Nance says, 'Oh, you are, Father; and I want Mother to be' (15). Mother never is, but the father who at first appears as the most pitiless tyrant becomes more sympathetic, until his and the book's last words announce the Head's arrogance, power and intellectual superiority but also his care and responsibility: 'I am here to give you a word when you need it. You are all at my hand to be taught' (276). Critics have remarked on Compton-Burnett's creation of tyrants who are appalling and unreformed but sometimes tolerable, perhaps likeable, even admirable, and in this book the dialogue between title and psychological action helps to explain them.

Duncan, called after a good king killed by the tyrant Macbeth, shows us how that house of which he is head is many things: household, family, property, territory, responsibility, duty, an inheritance received from ancestors and to be passed on to descendants – in all, an organism of which he is an organ, indispensable but not independent. He echoes the words of the title, obsessed, and possessed in more senses than one: there are times when he is clearly not an all-powerful individual, but depersonalised, a part of a whole as a head is part of a body. The common phrase 'house and head' is defamiliarised, the subtle and dynamic title making us see that this tyrant and patriarch has power but not absolute power, so is not absolutely corrupted. His identity and agency are taken over by the power of the house, which is made stranger, larger and animated, said, in a profound and creepy insight, to have 'room' to 'spread' its life (190).[8]

A Family and a Fortune (1939) once or twice echoes the title of this predecessor. Discussing a woman's authority, her aunt Matty suggests that Justine Edgeworth may 'remain in effect the head of the house' when her stepmother moves in (216), and though the word 'house' in this instance has an immediately domestic denotation, its scope is soon seen to be wider; elsewhere in the novel, it is used in the sense of a social and historic organism rather than a home or a building. This novel concentrates on inheritance and money, and family drama is central as all its members are changed more than once by the inheritance of a fortune which proves neither wholly fortunate nor unfortunate. As that fortune is announced, celebrated, shared, renounced, claimed, demanded, retrieved, denied and given again, in a variety of tones, emotions and rhetoric, every turn and twist of the unfolding tragi-comic drama wonderfully intricates the weave of expectation and surprise, like that in the Greek tragedy the novelist studied for her classics degree at Royal Holloway. The words 'fortunate', 'unfortunate' and 'fortune' are inconspicuously scattered about in conversation, their appearance seemingly casual, but the plot turns more emphatically and expansively on various kinds of fortune – a large sum of money, a stroke of luck and a stroke of ill-luck – and may remind us of the Roman goddess, Fortuna, the turning wheel, and any kind of Fate. Fortune in all senses is variously apportioned inside and sometimes outside the family, as that family and the fortune are dramatised in tense and shifting relationships, emphasised by the euphony and intelligence of the title.

At times, the abstract meanings resonate, but we are never allowed to forget real, serious money, and this novelist, always anxious about her own earned and inherited income and capital, makes play with brute particulars of the sums, values and denominations which make up our fortunes. 'How much?', the characters are all dying to know, especially when, for a variety of bad reasons, they insist that they are not, and there are running jokes about the generosity of receiving, the ambiguities of giving, the conscience of the rich, and the way percentages of a million – vaguely and wildly quoted in gossip or hearsay – all seem a lot and all seem the same.

The novel deals with the fortunes of love, and money affects personal relations: when Dudley, the unfortunate or fortunate heir to a fortune, expects to marry Maria, he has to take back his presents and promises; when he loses her to his brother, the family gets them back, joking away but taking it all seriously too. And as he jokingly impersonalises his situation, Dudley feels and expresses his submission to contingency in a way his author treats with a devastatingly clear vision. In *A House and Its Head*, Miles's resilient submissions led to his survival, but here Dudley's powerlessness brings him to breakdown, almost to death. This novelist, whose characters ignore politics, apart from a rare glance at a newspaper, can implicitly and dramatically show her awareness of the social environment. She does politics through psychology.

Another striking title heads *Elders and Betters* (1944), of whose irony Elizabeth Bowen[9] said, 'everyone in this novel is the same age, and nobody is admirable.' I see what she means but the children, though not always kind, do less damage than the adults, and their private religion is the only one in all the novels that is not unsympathetic, stupid or hypocritical. For reasons obvious to readers Compton-Burnett would have found congenial, she makes it child's play, but quietly; we cannot be sure if it is faith as well as game. The novel is distinguished by her worst villain, Anna Donne, the only liar and killer in the novels who is never found out, except by the reader. Certainly, these elders are not anyone's betters, as the traditional phrase can imply or deny, used straight-faced or ironically, and certainly not better than the novel's children. Like 'the way of the world' and 'the last and the first', the common phrase used for the title of one book crops up in other books, and in the earlier *Pastors and Masters* a clergyman humorously refers to his elder sister and slightly older wife as 'my elders and betters' (29). The ambiguous hendiadys was not invented by the author but cleverly borrowed from the genius of the language; the riddling and mind-shuttling compression of the figure makes it work brilliantly as a title.

Manservant and Maidservant (1947), a favourite with its author,[10] has an unusual title, as I have said, which seems to have a lopsided or obscure reference to its text. It is certainly a title that directs our attention to the below-stairs action, which, though shared with upstairs, occupies more space than in any other novel, and whose servant characters – Mrs Selden, the pious singing cook with a style; Miriam, the round, red, con- tented orphan with a future; and George, the workhouse-born footman with a wit – are developed characters, socially rooted in disadvantage but free spirits – or almost. They are presided over by the butler, Bullivant, the servant as hero, as central as the famous manservants in Henry James, Wodehouse and Ishiguro. The title is anticipated at the beginning of *Men and Wives*, when Godfrey Haslam, in conversation with his butler, lists 'my menservants and my maidservants' with objects and people which are his pride and joy (8).

At first, neither the similarity nor the difference between the sexes seems dominant but once we have become used to the title's emphasis, and let it direct our attention not only below stairs but to the part played by the servants upstairs, and when the politics of service comes under discussion, that title switches and deepens its meaning to move from the literal to the metonymic. As in Mozart's even more class-conscious *Marriage of Figaro*, we come to see that maidservant, manservant, mistress and master are alike as well as different. This does not make us approve the class divisions, though it sometimes helps the underlings to tolerate them. And once we hear someone saying everyone is a servant, I think we can see the point of suggesting a gender, not class, divide in the title.

In this novel everyone is a servant in some way or other, though perhaps not in the way approved by Bullivant, appropriately made to make this explicit in his masterful and also subservient fashion. His junior, George, who, like most servants in this and the other novels, makes no bones about deploring his status, especially when master or mistress tries to soothe or flatter, declares, 'All the world is not a servant', and Bullivant's eloquent disagreement, with its nice, plausible touch of sentimental royalism, is clearly a class-comforting defence of the status quo. He can be cynical about the joys of service when talking to his master but not when instructing his dependent pupil: 'Pardon me, George . . . all the world is. There is no one, from the first to the last, who does not serve in some way the stratum above himself. Even the Queen is the servant of the State' (198).

Compton-Burnett's attitudes to class and service were conservative, but when she came to imagine the effects of class and service on character she was neither sentimental nor illiberal. The unusual title – certainly not one the common reader would have chosen – was giving all its space to one class, and not dividing but bracketing manservant and maidservant, for a good reason. The apparent discrepancy between title and theme works well, nudging us go on asking questions and play our active part in the retardation Goethe thought essential to good narrative. The class-comforting defence of servitude recurs in *The Mighty and Their Fall* (1961) when the butler boasts, 'I am glad I am not under anyone' and the novelist uses upper case to make the sanctimonious cook extend the scope of his preposition, 'We are all under Someone' (112).

Two Worlds and Their Ways (1949) is a title which perfectly introduces and fits a story in which home and school are contrasted and evaluated, in ways which force us into ironic and relativist judgements of nurture and nature, cause and effect. The two worlds – made two by metaphor – are frequently so called, but Compton-Burnett has an easy hand with her keywords, and 'world' is often also used literally, in a general sense, as in 'The world would be a poorer place' (36); 'Much of what is done in the world is begun as a means to live' (73); and 'I do not claim to be a person who oils the wheels of the world' (286). It is used in a common metonymy to describe worldliness: one of the three heads of the girls' school, who seems unworldly, is revealed as not living 'apart from the world' (116); a schoolmaster mentions his 'family who see me as a worldly success' (183); and another, who has spent an experimental term teaching, observes, 'I don't think I shall ever be a man of the world again' and 'I shall see people's problems beneath the surface. And that is the last thing a man of the world does' (186–7). It is used in scathing comments about reality and fantasy: 'A fairy sphere . . . This hard, unhappy human world' and 'Yes, hers is the fairy world . . . I hope the rain of gold and precious stones will not change into one of toads and snakes' (219–20). As I said, it is a title which echoes a phrase from other novels: *More Women than Men* (1933), where clever Felix ponders the cliché and metaphor, 'a school is a miniature world', to say, 'That is just what it is not' and elaborates, 'My father is a man of the world. It is little, unnatural corners of the world that appeal to me' (41–2). It also appears in *A Family and a Fortune* (1939), which has 'It is the way of the world' (10), and *Manservant and Maidservant* (1947), which talks of 'the ways of the world' (202). It is itself echoed in *Darkness and Day* (1951): 'The way of the world is the opposite' (136). It is a common phrase which Compton-Burnett makes uncommonly telling, but her repetitions of course also echo *The Way of the World*, and her witty fluent dynamic is very like Congreve's; she must have loved dialogues like the contractual discussion of marriage between Millament and Mirabel, where sophisticated wit elegantly cools and controls passionate desire. Like Mozart's *Così fan tutte*, the title of the Restoration play has an air of worldly and humane nonchalance, encouraging us to be tolerant rather than judgemental while distinguishing better and worse, and there is an echo of this insouciance in the worlds and ways of the novel's title.

Most importantly, Compton-Burnett's metaphorical version alerts us to comparisons explicitly made by characters in the discussions about home education and school, joined by family, governess, school-teachers and most conspicuously the children who express views before, during and after they experience the two worlds, but from time to time pointedly responding to the title. For instance, we have, 'I should like to see the world of school from a different angle and know why it is called a world' (52); 'you will wait and let the new world break upon you in all its unexpectedness' (67); 'her home world' (130); 'It is strange that three places, that were really kind, should bring us to such misery. Because our home and both the schools are really gentle worlds' (210); describing what Clemence feels as the 'gulf between the words (sic)[11] of school and home, the ignorance in each of the other', which makes her 'wonder she had ever thought she could live between them' (269); and once using the word in the common phrase, 'You would not like to have the best of both worlds?' (305). At the end, the child protagonists sum up their experience – and the main theme, seeing home and school as places that cannot understand each other, and homes as places that can never be understood: 'To think there are thousands of them, all over the world!' (306).

If we come to a conclusion before the end, we must think again, as the title's meaning is ironically demonstrated and enlarged by an action in which school-nurture corrupts the children but home-nurture turns out to have corrupted their equally weak and dishonest parents – unless, of course, as the novel also suggests, it is not nurture but nature. The title makes us sociologists and psychologists, in a study of contrasted environments which turn out to justify that big word, 'world'. The emphasis on subject sometimes seems clear and simple, and sometimes is, but some titles do not ever seem simple. This one has a large range.

This is also true of *Darkness and Day* (1951)[12]; the unusually imagistic title announces metaphor, which, like all metaphor, acts as a question. We expect to search and interpret its meanings, and we do, but its significance is only gradually unfolded. On the first page, a metaphor of sunlight and the word 'today' are connected to the title, beginning a pattern more insistent than image recurrences in the other novels, articulated by characters who speak literally and figuratively of night and day, dusk, shadows, clouds and light. The narrator and her people make pictures; a child not afraid of 'the dark' but of 'pieces of light and darkness' (87), and another seen as 'a shadow' sneaking upstairs (118), are images lit and shadowed by the darkness and day of the title.

The darkness first images Bridget's and Edmund's belief that their marriage is incestuous, with the psychological and social effects of horror, shame and sexual inhibition, all deepening as the story spreads to people apparently leading more ordinary and less clouded lives. Sometimes characters reflect on their own use of image, as when Edmund develops and renews a recurring metaphor: 'The cloud must be lighter as it spreads . . . But it must spread no further,' which the more analytic and introspective Bridget wants to change: 'A cloud is the word we use. It seems a strange one. The trouble is at the base of our lives, at the root of the children's being' (113). Then 'cloud' and 'clouded' turn up as dead metaphors in the commonplace of conversation as Bartle, the 'boy', gloats, 'This is the cloud and the mystery' (141), and Fanshawe, the children's nanny, apologises, 'I am sorry a cloud has been cast, and that I was the unwilling instrument' (145). The articulate servants take part, without condescension by their author, in the subtle, playful analysis of language that is one of the delights of the novels.

The imagery of title and text nudges us towards questions and answers, when the day that clears the first darkness begins to darken again, as days do. But is the day all that bright and the darkness all that dark? The dark and the day are outside us and inside, and the relation between the two, causal and rhetorical, is not always clear. Dead metaphors revive and die again. There are many darknesses and lights, clouds and shadows, and the cycle only comes to a stop with the very last page, in an action where everyone is in the dark in some way, about some things. The exceptions are two wise women, the grandmother and the cook, who know the dark truth, though it is not entirely dark; but while a vibrant ending brings enlightenment and resolution to them, and their relationship is changed for good, some things must be kept dark from others. For everyone to survive, their day depends on darkness. Moreover, darkness and day exist together, at the same time, as they cannot in real time.

Reversing Carlyle's title, *The Present and the Past* (1953), presents us from the start with cover-all, general meanings which allow for no such development of title relevance, though the book raises philosophical questions about the relationship of past and present which we might not ponder without that title's prodding. It points straightforwardly to the single plot about a man whose ex-wife and present wife meet, but there are moments when the relation between past and present is abstracted and thrown into high relief by the title's emphasis. Catherine, the first wife, speaks to her husband after a gap of nine years and he supposes,

in banal phrase, that she 'would be surprised' to see their elder son
Fabian 'now', to get her thoughtful reply, 'As a boy of thirteen? No,
that is how I think of him'. After a further commonplace, 'So we are to
let the dead past bury its dead?', she replies again with her customary
care, 'The past is dead . . . It has no dead to bury. My sons' lives are
young' (73). Guided by the title to notice the 'now' and the 'past', we
give the exchange special attention.

We see characters thinking about time in a way we would probably
not notice without the title's nudge: for instance, Cassius speaks of the
passing of time in an unthinking cliché, 'Take each day as it comes', urg-
ing his son Fabian to think about the banal phrase and beyond it, 'Guy
could never do that', and his wife too, 'And neither could I. Life is not
a matter of days. Each one is part of the whole' (95), both responding
freshly to the title. On another occasion, more thoughtfully, using banal
and less banal phrases, Cassius complains, 'The past was somehow too
much for me. It rose up and overwhelmed me,' and his father responds
to the active metaphor 'rose up': 'The past would be too much for any
of us, if it did not stay in its place' (111).

The title is a quiet, unobtrusive monitor, and its magnetising effect
can work without such overt verbal pressure, as, for instance, when
his father, wife, sons and daughter realise that they are still feeling for
Cassius after his death. The father can be consoled by the past, in the
present: 'I was with him . . . It is my drop of comfort, and I need not do
without it' (166). The wife looks back and imagines her husband dead
but also alive: 'Would Cassius be glad to be missed so much?' (165).
The children are surprised by their own new response and judgement:
'It seems that a person's dying makes you know more about him' (178).
The psychology of bereavement has familiar features but it is given new
particularities in the development of past emotions and relationships.
These comments are dynamic in a way which propels the action towards
and beyond the conclusion. Compton-Burnett's endings are usually
excellent, but this one is unusual, I think, in its importance and its
muteness, surely unguessable.

The relation of abstract title to character and action in *A Father and
His Fate* (1957) works in much the same way, pointing obviously and
superficially to the varied fates – fortunes, crises, adventures – experienced by Miles, the demanding patriarch, and more complexly to the
responses of his chameleon-like character. Though he has to submit to
external exigency – shipwreck, the apparent drowning of his wife, the
exciting charm and erotic response of his heir's betrothed, his wife's

unexpected resurrection, his ex-lover's persistence – he accepts each crisis and challenge as his fate, then gives each one up, taking the line of least resistance, always submitting with a sense of destiny which is self-flattering, egocentric, weakly flexible and exhilaratingly successful.

A tyrannical character, powerful and yet conveniently weak in identity, he accepts his fate fatalistically. His doubled performance as a King Lear trying out the three daughters is a clue to both his histrionic adaptability and his survival; when the trials fail, he accepts failure with un-Lear-like complacency. He will never go mad or doubt his identity. He says he is 'destined not to live as other men' (145) and one of his daughters observes the grandiose style, 'So it was something as dignified as destiny' (145). He is proud of being good father, bad father, good widower, virile lover and restored husband, on the last page preparing to be a grandfather to his own child and 'hoping' for his real grand-children, so when the wise, choric character, Miss Gibbon, responds with the last line, 'I daresay he is!', her laconic, amused acquiescence is eloquent (214). There is still another part he can play. His eldest daughter has told him, 'You are the character of the story' (156), and he is, but he is many characters, and sometimes characterless, and in future may be different characters. Once again, the end pushes us beyond itself.

Miles's very lack of identity puts the other strong characters in the shade, even determined egoists like Verena, his young lover; Eliza, his self-regarding sister-in-law; and Constance, his complacent, pious daughter. They are powerful and try to make their fate, and lose; he bows to it, and wins. Like his children and nephews, observers of it all, we are appalled, passive, reluctantly admiring the tyrant. He is the master of his fate – never quoted, the phrase echoes through the novel – because he lets it master him. In all its guises, it is a comic fate, not a tragic one, and the title alerts us to his survivals and our response.

John Preston, one of the few critics to comment in detail on a title, says of *A Heritage and Its History* (1959), 'The "heritage" gives a hold on the "civilised" world; its "history", its continuity, is a way of defying death.'[13] Perhaps this interpretation over-dignifies the motives and passions dramatised and implicitly analysed in Simon, the man at the centre of the novel's highly concentrated inner and outer action. His ruling passion is an obsessive desire for the heritage but his sexual susceptibility almost disinherits him, and for years thwarts and corrupts his relationships with his family, especially his children. The novel is one of the most searching of the author's psychological studies, interioris-ing the actions of adultery, illegitimacy and threatened incest which are followed through a long development, or deterioration, but also showing the powerful agents of class, money and property shaping the struggles of the fathers and their descendants. The word 'history' emphasises this unusually prolonged time-span, formed for a negative *Bildungsroman*. Simon's step-mother, Rhoda, by whom he has a child (sexual intercourse is as fertile for Compton-Burnett's people as for Zeus), says, 'We know the natural life beneath,' but that natural life is analysed in a socially specified environment, its action artfully ironic and comic, teasing us on the verge of tragedy right to the end.

The Mighty and Their Fall (1961) was a title that did not satisfy Compton-Burnett, as we hear from Cicely Grieg,[14] the friend and admirer who typed all her novels after *A House and Its Head*; when asked to suggest another title, she came up with *The Just and the Unjust,* though in the end the original phrase, used jokingly by the butler and cook on the last page, was kept. Burkhart liked it for its irony; he observes that the fallen hero, Ninian, stronger and more unscrupulous than Miles but equally flexible, 'has not learned from the experience; he has not seemed to need to learn' and 'though the mighty may fall, they sustain no damage' (127).[15] This outcome is typical of Compton-Burnett's imaginative tolerance, as she makes us witness and ponder expected and unexpected kinds and consequences of might and fall, alerting us to a divergence from traditional tragedy involving a fall from greatness, as she knew from Greek drama and Aristotle. Her dissatisfaction seems significant: she was using a biblical title ironically pointing to comic genre and revisionary ethic, appropriating a phrase from the great elegy for Jonathan in the Book of Samuel, a varied heartbroken refrain and loving lamentation remote from the unheroic actions and untragic shortfalls in the novel: 'How are the mighty fallen in the midst of the battle! O Jonathan, thou wast slain in thine high places' (1 Samuel 10: 25); and 'How are the mighty fallen and the weapons of war perished! The beauty of Israel is slain upon thy high places: how are the mighty fallen!' (1 Samuel 10: 27). Was she dissatisfied with her title because of her sensitivity to words and cadences, a deep familiarity with her source, its tragic passions a far cry from the culture, subjects and language of her cool and comic art in this novel?

Another very different metaphorical and questioning title is *A God and His Gifts* (1963). What kind of God is this god and what kind of gifts does he get and give? The title's appropriation of godhead reminds us at the start that the novelist likes a touch of blasphemy. She may have felt uneasy about quoting the lament for Jonathan but she was a creative atheist, quietly, seriously and amusedly complicit with the irreligious reader. Her atheism, like her sexual liberation and tolerance, is effective and enjoyable because it is understated or unstated, casual-sounding, never strident or argumentative. She does not make a philosophical or historical case because she takes it for granted that intelligent readers agree with her and understand her. One of her best clerics, Oscar Jekyll in *A House and Its Head,* knows that those who do not disbelieve will not notice his heterodoxy or understand his hard subtle sermons because they are dunces. They never fail him. The call for reason is always there.

The gifts turn out to be active, given boastfully and demandingly, for better and for worse, by Hereward, another persistent but adaptable patriarch. Like Miles and Ninian, he knows how to be passive, excusing or impersonalising his own human vainglory. If Compton-Burnett revered religious poetry and was saturated in the Bible, she did not respect any gods, Christian or pre-Christian. In this novel, the tenor of the comparison changes places with the vehicle, taking us from a powerful, human father – breadwinner, novelist, tyrant, thief, liar, boss and bully – to other gods, the dangerously gift-bearing Greek gods of Olympus, especially lecherous and polyphiloprogenitive Zeus, Jehovah, and Our Father in Heaven emerging as generous and destructive role models. Beware not only Greek but all gods bearing gifts.

Compton-Burnett's titles usually turn out to be complexly purposive; some novels explore themes not foreshadowed or underlined in the titles and nearly all have more in them than the titles suggest. The titles of *Men and Wives* (1931), *Daughters and Sons* (1937), *Parents and Children* (1941) and *Mother and Son* (1955) are, like *Brothers and Sisters,* announcing family subjects, and though Burkhart suggests that the five titles in this group are interchangeable,[16] on close examination they turn out to do more than meet the eye that made this judgement. *Men and Wives* is not a phrase in common use and the actual title never appears in the text; the closest we come to it is at the end, when Godfrey Haslam, condemned to perpetual widowerhood by his wife's will, sentimentally recalls 'all the years we had lived together as man and wife' (287). Most of its characters are or have been married; there are three widowers, three divorced spouses, six unmarried men and women; and separations of husbands and wives are frequent and central, but at the centre of the disturbing and violent psychological action is the relationship between a mother and her children. *Men and Wives* is the only title in the œuvre which might be changed for other titles referring to family relations, and which, like *Manservant and Maidservant*, does not impress itself on the whole novel.

All the titles in this family group, except *Men and Wives* and *Daughters and Sons*, are familiar, easy-running locutions introduced unobtrusively in the course of narrative and dialogue. *Daughters and Sons* conspicuously reverses the usual noun order, *Sons and Daughters*, questioning gender precedence. Like *Men and Wives*, it is not familiar to us in conversation and would be conspicuous if it were used in narrative or dialogue, and it is not. On three out of four occasions when they are verbally linked, the sons and daughters are in the usual order: 'her son and daughter' (87), 'son and daughter' (278), and the significant question, 'Why do women think of men? Why do mothers think of sons, when they have their daughters?' (221), which draws attention to the reversal in the title and to its significance. It is a novel where daughters are more powerful and central than sons.

Parents and Children is a familiar phrase, but though the novel frequently uses the words 'parents' and 'children', it never repeats the title's phrase. The relationships of siblings, grandparents, man and wife are important, but there is no doubt that the good parenting of Fulbert Sullivan and the bad parenting of his wife, Eleanor, are central, individually and subtly dramatised in the married couple and the nine wonderful child characters. The title draws attention to this, not only in the obvious places, like Eleanor's active but insensitive maternal affections, but also in counter-examples, like the sceptical, childless woman Hope's attitude to her stepchildren and her friends' children. The title also points to the elegant balance of the novel's form; guided by its emphasis, we notice that the book begins and ends with talk of parents and children, and appreciate the way the last sentence marks closeness and distance as an illegitimate daughter stands at her window and her father 'gave her a glance as he passed, and raised his hat and walked on' (318).

Mother and Son divides action and interest between a mothered and fathered family and a less conventional one: though Rosebery, the mother's boy, is a central figure who is clearly motivated by the effects of a mutual excessive love, this is not a dynamic and developing action, like the pleasant drama of the all-woman household with which it is contrasted. This title presides more lightly over its novel, more simply and obviously describing conflicts and secrets of sibling relations, paternities, maternities and adulteries. It could easily have had another title, without loss, or even with gain, being what Compton-Burnett often jokingly questioned: the exception which proves the rule.

The Last and the First was the last novel. Dishevelled and unfinished, it was revised and edited[17] from 'thirteen or fourteen' exercise books by the author's friends, Elizabeth Sprigge and Cicely Grieg. Grieg describes the choice of title:

Elizabeth Sprigge . . . had just finished reading as much as she could of that last disordered manuscript. She said: 'The last shall be first, and the first last,' one of Ivy's last sentences. Without saying so we both thought it might make a good title.[18]

Their title derives from Christ's rebuke to his disciples as they jostle for a good place in the house of which his Father is Head. Unlike *The Mighty and Their Fall*, the title the author chose but did not like, this one she did not choose sounds no dissonance, risks no bathos or disrespect, and presides easily over the text: 'But many that are first shall be last; and the last shall be first'; 'So the last shall be first, and the first last: for many be called, but few chosen'[19]; 'And he sat down, and called the twelve, and saith unto them, If any man desire to be first, the same shall be last of all, and servant of all', and 'But many that are first shall be last; and the last first.'[20]

Devised to conform to the series, the title echoes earlier novels. Mr Merry of *Pastors and Masters* is buttering up the mother of a prospective pupil – 'your boy . . . the first too, isn't he? Bless him, yes' (15) – and Richard Bumpus, pretending he is writing a new novel, really his old one, asks Nicholas Herrick, wriggling out of reading his purloined novel, really Bumpus's, 'Why should the first be last, and the last first?' (72). In *Men and Wives*, there is a joke about first and last going into dinner (95), and in *A Father and His Fate* the pretentious Miles also jokes about dining precedence, 'The first shall be last and the last first', but is 'not quite sure of his meaning' (164). In *Manservant and Maidservant*, Bullivant says we are all servants, 'from the first to the last' (198). In the last but one novel, *A God and His Gifts*, the eldest son, Salomon's, 'The first shall be last, and the last first' (99), leads to the disclosure of the illegitimate last child's identity. The author did not know *The Last and the First* would be her last book – though she must have had an inkling – so the magnificent, stern words became a playful, allusive title she would have enjoyed, as they echo all these key passages, including the last sentence of *The Last and the First* itself, the last novel and the one she did not finish: 'How the first can be last, and the last first!' (139), in a voice from the past and from beyond the tomb.

Ivy Compton-Burnett's titles are part of the text, but also outside it and above it, signals to reader and signatures of the artist.

Notes

1. Samuel Taylor Coleridge, *Shakespearean Criticism*, 107.
2. The first novel, *Dolores*, is eponymous, and the nineteenth, *The Last and the First*, was given its title by Elizabeth Sprigge and Cicely Grieg: see Grieg, *Ivy Compton-Burnett: A Memoir*.
3. 'Hendiadys': the combination of two nouns or adjectives to express a single idea, where you usually see an adjective qualifying a noun, or adverb qualifying an adjective. The *Princeton Encyclopaedia of Poetry and Poetics* gives a well-known example from Virgil's *Georgics*, 'we drink from cups and gold' (instead of 'golden cups'), and 'nice and warm' (instead of 'nicely warm'). My favourite is Shakespeare's 'dark backward and abysm of time', with the extra touch of 'dark' to describe both 'backward' and 'abysm' (*The Tempest*, I, ii). Hendiadys removes the subordination of qualifier, letting us dwell on and appreciate the gold of those drinking cups, the niceness of that warmth, and feel vast space behind and beneath in our memory of the past. The traditional phrase, 'elders and betters', outrageously proposes, or ironically subverts the proposal, that to be the elder is to be the better.
4. Edward Sackville-West, 'Ladies Whose Bright Pens', in *The Art of I. Compton-Burnett*, ed. Burkhart, 107.
5. See Michael Millgate, 'Interview with Miss Compton-Burnett', in *The Art of I. Compton-Burnett*, ed. Burkhart, 40–1.
6. 'A soft spot': see Millgate, 'Interview with Miss Compton-Burnett', in *The Art of I. Compton-Burnett*, ed. Burkhart, 42.
7. Quotations from Ivy Compton-Burnett are from *The Novels of I. Compton-Burnett*, the Limited Edition of 500 copies produced posthumously, and at the author's request excluding *Dolores*. Dates of novels are given where development seems involved in my discussion.
8. See Chapter 5 for a full discussion of this subject.
9. Elizabeth Bowen, 'Elders and Betters', in *The Art of I. Compton-Burnett*, ed. Burkhart, 62.
10. 'A favourite with its author': see Millgate, 'Interview with Miss Compton-Burnett', in *The Art of I. Compton-Burnett*, ed. Burkhart, 42.
11. In the 1972 limited edition, 'words' for 'worlds' is one of many misprints.
12. For a full discussion see Chapter 10.
13. John Preston, 'Review of *A Heritage and Its History*', in *The Art of I. Compton-Burnett*, ed. Burkhart, 73.
14. Cicely Grieg, *Ivy Compton-Burnett: A Memoir*, 128.

15. Charles Burkhart, *I. Compton-Burnett*, 207.
16. Ibid. 25.
17. There are two retentions of what could be the author's unrevised mistakes in *The Last and the First*: a repeated episode of refusing fat at breakfast (Chapters 1 and 2) and a repeated reference to a carpenter repairing a staircase (Chapters 1 and 3). The holograph notebooks (British Library, MS 57851 A-L: 1964–1969) shed no light on the problem.
18. Grieg, *Ivy Compton-Burnett: A Memoir*, 128.
19. Robert Carroll and Stephen Prickett (eds), *The Bible: Authorized King James Version* (Oxford: Oxford University Press, 2008), Matthew 19: 30 and 20: 16.
20. Ibid. Mark 9: 31 and 10: 34.

Chapter 2

Making Conversation

Ivy Compton-Burnett's genre is the Conversation Novel,[1] and her interest in minds, feelings and behaviour is inseparable from her interest in the way we talk to each other. Her novels use conversation and are about conversation, in an original and demanding way. At its best the talk is witty, dynamic and subtly self-analytic, an earnest and comic scrutiny of words, phrases and the interplay of speech, self-conscious enough to become a brilliant meta-language.

She did not want to write plays because she needed the elasticity of a novel but her conversation form, which stepped 'into the bounds of drama',[2] puts pressure on the reader. She makes sparing use of interior monologue, in direct or indirect style, presenting not streams of consciousness but streams of talk, from which we infer what is going on inside her characters. The talk often proceeds without speakers being named, and though we can identify them by style or content, re-reading may be necessary; they may be distinguished by idiolect but because, like all literary creatures, they use variations of their novelist's style, we may have to think before we know who is speaking. Less often observed is an occasional break in sequence. In most novels each statement or question is immediately followed by response, but Compton-Burnett's conversation may move backward and forward in a way more common in life than novels; when four people talk, the last may reply not to the third but the first. The most prominent feature is the scrutiny of one speaker's speech by another, a consistent and dynamic nit-picking. Sometimes this is simply argumentative, as when Emily in *Pastors and Masters* offends a conventional Christian by calling God one of the best characters in fiction, or the dogmatic Constance and her cousin in *A Father and His Fate* disagree about immortality, or mother and child in *Parents and Children* quarrel about the rights and wrongs of opening somebody else's letter. More distinctive is a refusal to let language pass, as we do all the time in phatic communion, routine in-group language and dead metaphor. Life is too short to scrutinise every word but art can slow it up, and Compton-Burnett's art certainly does.

She highlights the talk of relations and friends in an intimate group, occasionally in dialogue. It is almost always family conversation, never the impassioned exchange of lovers so common in novels: think of Anne Elliot and Wentworth in *Persuasion*, Dorothea and Ladislaw in *Middlemarch*, Paul Morel and his mother in *Sons and Lovers*. Compton-Burnett's talk typically takes place in a domestic space, like dining-room, drawing-room, kitchen, nursery or school-room, but may move outside to a public stage, like church, village hall, school, common-room. There are few outdoor scenes, though people sometimes observe each other through a window as they walk in a garden, and may linger outside neighbours' houses, or very occasionally go for walks on roads or fields which are never described. These are indoor novels with public conversation. Pascal said human beings find it hard to be alone in a room, and Compton-Burnett's people are never seen alone in theirs – in *A Family and a Fortune* Clement has to let people into his bedroom because his uncle collapses outside, and he is revealed as a miser. There are two occasions when lovers talk alone: Felix and Jonathan in *More Women than Men*, and Hereward and Rosa in *A God and His Gifts*. There are two occasions when we know where lovers have made love: a bedroom in *A Father and His Fate*, where tell-tale garments are found in a chest-of-drawers, and a drawing-room in *A House and Its Head*.

In *Dolores* there is a good deal of comment about language, but only one scene, set in a college common-room, concentrates on conversation and makes rhetoric self-analytic:

'Do any of you remember when you first realised that things in books need not be true?' said Miss Cliff, with the half-philosophising interest in her kind, which was one of her characteristics. 'Do you remember feeling the ground you were used to walk upon, slipping from under your feet, and a mist of scepticism rising around you?'

A lady who was standing apart came forward to join in the talk. She was a Frenchwoman, over fifty, with a sallow, clever face, and sad brown eyes which lighted with her smile; who had led a difficult life in the land of her forced adoption, and lived with its daughters, feeling that she owed it no gratitude.

'I imagine most of us had that experience at an early stage for such power of metaphor to be born,' she said.

'I did not mean the metaphors to be quoted from childish reflections,' said Miss Cliff. 'I was putting a childish experience into unchildish language. But I remember the experience itself so well. It marks off a chapter in my life for me.'

'Yes; we have so much faith as children' ... 'I daresay we could all mark off the chapters in our lives by loss of faith in something.' ...

...

'It seems we can mark age by steps in scepticism' ... 'It would be a help to our curiosity on both, to remember they correspond.'

'It would be a very good way of guessing people's ages ... We should simply have to start some disputed topics; and having discovered the doubted points, calculate the chapters marked off.' (99–101)[3]

(After the second paragraph, I omit stage directions, which get fewer in the novels which follow.)

This exchange between colleagues talking in metaphor about metaphor in a mildly amusing way is on the verge of action, with minor characters. The novel's last chapter (21) is set in the same room with the same choric group, with the addition of Dolores, but there is no interplay or scrutiny of lexis and rhetoric, and the talk is about marrying and not marrying, in ironic conclusion to Dolores's sad history.

In *Pastors and Masters*, the conversational to-and-fro runs through the novel, but it is not yet demandingly concentrated or self-conscious. Neither is the action: it is not a novel with a psychological centre. There are full stage directions, but now and then we must attend closely to the words used and re-used. In this typical snatch of acerbic conversation the speakers are talking about the charitable Miss Lydia, just off to cancel a meeting with her 'dear men things', saying she did not often fail men: 'I am different with women' but 'men don't often elude me.'

'I feel I do elude Lyddie,' said Emily. 'I am always having proof that I am the average woman' ...

'She seems very pleased with not failing with men, and failing with women,' said Theresa. 'It would be better not to fail with either.'

'No, if you think a minute, not so good,' said Emily. 'Not so nice, anyway.'

'I don't think myself so good,' said Bumpus. 'Much less good, of course.'

'It is something not to fail with one, my dear,' said Mr Fletcher.

'I knew you would say that, Peter,' said Theresa. 'You self-righteous, obvious old man. I did not say it was not.' (33)

But by the time we get to the claustrophobic Stace household of *Brothers and Sisters*, conversation is in full swing, with the in-group chatter of Andrew, Dinah and Robin, children of incestuously married Sophia and Christian. Terribly constrained by their domineering and beautiful mother, as if more her possessions because of her double bond to the husband–brother, they are relaxed in her absence, released into truth-telling by intimacy and secrecy. Here they are looking at their grandfather's 'menacing' portrait and talking behind Sophia's back, where they cheekily use her Christian name. Andrew addresses their ancestor:

> 'Well, old man . . . so your choice of a subject was yourself! There would have been better stuff for the painter in Sophia.' . . .
> 'And enough of the same stuff,' said Dinah. 'He was perpetuated enough. Don't ask me to look at him.'
> 'I am not asking it,' said Andrew. 'There are some sights not fit for a woman.'
> 'Then the sight is not fit for either of you,' said Robin. 'To hear you use your tongue, Andrew! You are less of a man than Sophia.'
> 'But quite enough of a man,' said Dinah.
> 'Dinah and I are of the stuff that martyrs are made of,' said Andrew.
> 'You are more than that. You are martyrs,' said Robin. 'The weak part of martyrdom is, that it is so bad for other people.'
> 'I admit it brings out all that is worst in Sophia,' said Dinah.
> 'And I bring out the best in her. You must notice that,' said Robin.
> 'Yes,' said Dinah. 'It needs a very low person to bring out the best in others. I never thought martyrs were useful.'
> 'The highest things seldom are,' said Andrew. 'You would not have us as low as Robin?'
> 'No, but perhaps a little lower,' said Dinah. 'We are very high.'
> 'What passes me is, that Father has never got to know Sophia' . . . 'Day after day, year after year it goes on under his eyes, and he never sees it.'
> 'Not under his eyes, just away from them,' said Dinah. 'Don't you see how Sophia is on her guard?' (31–2)

Free to be amusing, complicit and disloyal, they are also attentive and analytic. Never a word passes without being held up for repetition and scrutiny: 'stuff', 'ask', 'sight', 'martyr', bringing out 'the best', 'low' and 'high', and 'under his eyes'. Nothing passes as commonplace. They cleverly pick up and pick on each other's well-worn phrases and dead metaphors, like 'the stuff martyrs are made of', taking off from them as with 'worst' and 'best', disagreeing with them as with 'under', accepting but modifying them as with 'perhaps a little lower', and revising them as with 'you are martyrs' and 'away'. They correct and are corrected in turn, their tone light, amused and affectionate, in a perfect example of collective thinking and talking which merges individual member in the group, in a style which serves the underlying and recurrent theme of the conditioning organism, here in the form of family.[4]

The awareness of language is there not only when children speak behind their mother's back. Like many such subdued or oppressed characters, they are given a surprising ability to talk back at the oppressor, and the questioning of words is aggressive as well as sympathetic, in its turn eliciting aggression, and reflection:

'When my life is broken, I don't want less from people who are supposed to love me. I need more.'

'You exact too much from people in that position,' said Andrew. 'You have gone too far.'

'Oh, do I? Well, I don't get it then,' said Sophia. 'I don't know what I have had, I am sure, to be taken so much into account.'

There was silence.

'What do I get?' said Sophia. 'What do I have, Andrew? It was you who spoke of my wanting too much.'

'Andrew did not say you had it. He said you claimed it,' said Dinah, trying to speak lightly. (152)

At times the conversation is more simply entertaining, as in a choric scene in *A House and Its Head* with Dulcia, the bouncy busybody, and her friends, the religiose Beatrice Fellowes and her sister, Miss Burtenshaw, a missionary who found the work too hard. Their style offers a crude contrast to the language of more sophisticated voices, as in Shakespeare's comic sub-plots, and here they are joined by Gretchen Jekyll and her rationalist clerical son, Oscar, critics of grandiloquence and banality. But all the characters, clever or stupid, turn their attention and ours to the words they use. So to words in general:

'Well, we have seen Sibyl turned from a maiden into a matron by a few magic words,' said Beatrice. 'Magic is of course hardly the word. I wonder if it will change her in other ways.'

'We can only hope not,' said Miss Burtenshaw, walking on in personal immunity from such risks.

'The wedding I should have liked to see,' said Dulcia, 'is Mr Edgeworth's to Miss Jekyll. Marriage rather, I would say. Wedding seems too

light a word for that union . . . I should have been a reverential witness
of their simple acquiescence at the altar. But it seemed it was not to be.'
   'It was not, as they wanted the ceremony private,' said Gretchen. (199)

An earlier conversation after the first Mrs Edgeworth's death is more
nuanced:

A week or two later the friends of Ellen Edgeworth came again to her
house.
   'This is our greatest pleasure for a long time,' said Mr Bode. 'It takes
us back to the old days.'
   'Father dear, that is just what it does not do. I thought you would get
a little further than this, without coming down.'
   'Well, we can't give everything up, because one of us is gone,' said
Gretchen, 'though it had better have been anyone else.'
   Beatrice looked round with smilingly contracted brows.
   'I am glad you see the joke,' said Gretchen, contriving that she no
longer saw it.
   'You may say it better have been yourself, Mother,' said Oscar. 'That
is as far as you must go.'
   'Enough of you think that, for it to go without saying.'
   'Ah, Mrs Jekyll, we would spare many people before you,' said Mr
Bode.
   'Now, careful, Father dear! In what sense are you using the word,
"spare"?'
   'In the sense in which he palpably used it,' said Almeric.
   'I don't think we can fairly accuse him of ambiguity,' said Beatrice.
   'I take sides against myself. Puns in all their degrees are odious.'
   'Let us check this process of elimination in time,' said Nance.
   'I am prepared to admit I am a much less needed person than Mrs
Edgeworth,' said Dulcia. 'And I am sure many people here would tell
themselves the same—Oh, what a thing to let slip, unawares! You dear,
dear things!' (100)

Not all the speakers are named here but occasion calls for some to
address each other by name. The talk differentiates various groupings
of family and acquaintance: Gretchen speaks to her son Oscar drily and
complicitly, as he replies to others frankly but with an irony they miss;
Dulcia speaks lightly but critically to her father, tactlessly and gushingly
to everyone; Almeric drily to his sister Dulcia; Nance coolly and wittily
to everyone. And all the discussion combines small-talk – some not so
small – with scrutiny of words.

The novel often starts with a dialogue then accumulates speakers, like these exchanges at breakfast in *A Heritage and Its History*. Here two brothers talk freely because they are close, and for the moment on their own. Characters unfold and exposition is implicit and unobtrusive. The dialogue begins with Walter joking about Simon not having his charm, and Simon voicing an obsession with his heritage:

'Uncle must leave everything to Father, before I even become the heir. It throws my life into an indefinite future, I never put it into words, but I carry a burden about with me.'

'It is praiseworthy not to put it into words. I wonder how it would be, if you did.'

'Words do not hasten things,' said Simon.

'No, or yours would have done so. Can it be that you have death in your heart? What a different thing from charm! To think of the gulf between us! I wonder if there is any outward sign of it.' (7)

And a little later:

'Well, charm should be on the surface,' said Simon. 'It has no hidden use.'

'It does what it can, one poor little portion amongst all that is without it. Strive on, Walter Challoner, and the charm you see in secret, you can reward openly.'

'There is none in being blasphemous,' said Simon, looking at the breakfast table.

'Simon, surely you are a modern man.'

'And none in ignoring conventions. And real charm should be unconscious.'

'No good quality is that. Good qualities involve effort. Without it they would not exist. Think of charity and tolerance. Even with it they exist uncertainly. But charm is perhaps more of the nature of a gift.' (8–9)

The complicit interplay is conspicuous, and when they go on, each character continues his train of thought, and personal tone, as well as answering: Simon says seriously that Walter 'is in a better position, pretending to be a poet' and Walter tells him seriously and jokingly not to speak 'like a member of my family. And just when you were being so different.' He advises Simon to emulate his own 'quiet courage', which will lead him 'onward'(8), but Simon says he is held back in everything, as in his wish to cut away the creeper 'smothering the house':

'When the place is mine, I shall have it cut away.'

'I did not mean you to be led as far onward as that. Uncle Edwin and Father would both have to die.'

'Well, people must die in the end.'

'Of course they must not. People are immortal. You must have noticed it. Indeed you betray that you have.'

'I wish I could think I was. My time will be too short to serve any purpose. And there are things I want to do so much.'

'Your voice broke with pardonable emotion. I had not met that before. So it is true that books are based on life. But you plan to do things when two people are dead. That proves you are immortal. It is they who are not.'

'It is what they seem to be. And older people would naturally die first.'

'Well, Nature is cruel . . .' (9)

'So it is true that books are based on life': there are many examples of this kind of play, fiction pretending it is fact comparing itself with fiction.

Their uncle, Edwin, arrives on his cue, 'Who is cruel?', and the conversation goes on to include him with a slight change of tone but not subject. Walter repeats his words in skilful modulation:

'Nature is cruel,' says Walter. 'She lets older people die before young, when they have a better right to live, as they have that to everything.'

'And have formed the habit of living,' said Simon, easily.

'Yes,' said Sir Edwin, glancing at him. 'But people may not die in order of age.'

'What did I tell you?' murmured Walter. 'You see he is immortal. Or anyway he sees it.' (9)

The stage directions – 'easily', 'glancing at him' and 'murmured' – probably make us re-read. The talk proceeds fluently and smoothly but each speaker attends to his own words and those of the others, and we must attend also, moving to and fro, following continuities and recapitulations. The men agree and disagree, lightly but with undertones. The young men's father, Hamish, enters on the cue of the word 'sixty': 'Here is someone else over sixty. It is a common thing.' He shows a different idiolect and is humorous in his way. Walter keeps murmuring, heard and overheard, Sir Edwin admonishes Simon for the poor habit of looking past other people's lives, the group is joined by their mother, picking up the word 'habit', and they tell her the talk started with the creeper. When the butler comes in, she asks Deakin if he knows the name of the creeper and he mentions 'two Latin words in an even tone', words interestingly excluded from the conversation in which Deakin plays a most articulate part, with the central image branching out:

'What do you feel about the creeper itself, Deakin? . . . You would not like to see it go?'
  'Well, ma'am, it would be a piece of life gone. But we are used to yielding it, little by little.'
  'I never become so,' said Hamish. 'Not even as I yield it more fully. I am always surprised by the lowering cloud.'
  'And we cannot depend on the silver lining, sir,' said Deakin. 'I have seen many clouds without it.'
  'I have never seen one with it,' said Walter. 'My clouds have been so very black.'
  'Well, the lighter the lining, sir, the darker the cloud may seem.' (13–14)

Julia says Deakin prides himself on pessimism; Walter praises his subtle talking; Deakin replies, 'Well, sir, there may be a tendency. And I have had examples'; Simon says, 'I could never copy anyone'; and the butler corrects him – 'Copy was not a word I employed, sir' (14). The exchange by masters and servants speaks for itself, in courtesies, condescensions and comparisons of language. There are several subjects in the serial conversation at breakfast, always explicitly and implicitly including language itself.

Linguistic scrutiny is adapted with flexibility. Here is a conversation from *A God and His Gifts,* one of the late novels described by Burkhart as 'existing in their dialogue, which becomes ever more incisively intelligent and compressed and subtle', and 'in themselves a concrete music'.[5] It is a conversation between Ada, the woman Hereward Egerton will marry, her sister Emmeline and their aunt Penelope, individualising character and mind, preparing action and plot:

'A little learning is a dangerous thing,' said Emmeline. 'And I should never have much. So perhaps I am better without it.'
  'Better than many of us, I believe,' said her aunt, smiling.
  'You are right, Aunt Penelope,' said Ada. 'It is large of you to see it. Ah, the old sayings are the best. Their wisdom never wears out. "A little learning" and the rest. "He does much who does a little well." They hold the truth.'
  'Perhaps the surface of it. I think not always more. When someone

does a little well, that is what he does. And very little it can be. Is there more truth in the theory of a great failure?'

'There may be. And perhaps a little truth in that of the small one. I must hope there is, as that is what I shall be. I feel it more when I talk to you, and glimpse the something beyond myself. But I remain an advocate of sayings. They give us wisdom in a nutshell. And that is what we need.'

'There can't be room for much in one,' said Emmeline. (31)

The conversation economises on name directions, making us work out speaker from speech. There is no sharing and stimulus, though the talk is affectionate. The characters speak thoughtfully but simply, and on a simple subject, quoting a familiar verse and two maxims. But we are made to think about language. These are Compton-Burnett characters, and all speak smoothly and neatly, but Ada is revealed by contrast: she is not analytic, content to accept 'the sayings' as wisdom, to use one herself, 'in a nutshell', and to call Pope's phrase from the *Essay on Criticism* 'a saying'. But she has some self-knowledge. In the previous chapter we have met Hereward, the man who intends to marry her, talking to the woman he first wanted to marry, and also read her language in the context of his style and mind.

As befits a god, Hereward says the first words – the 'fiat' – of *A God and His Gifts*, beginning one of the most austere conversations in the novels, in an exceptional scene which proves the 'rule' that they never show intimate talk between lovers. An amorous history is told in a brief dialogue:

'I will ask you once more. It is the last time. Will you or will you not?'

'I will not. It is also the last time. It must be the last.'

'You will not give me your reasons?'

'I will give you one. You have too much. Your house and your land. Your parents and your sister. Your sister who is also your friend. Your work and your growing name. I like things to be on a moderate scale. To have them in my hands and not be held by them.'

'That is not the only reason. There must be a deeper reason.'

'There is. And it may be deep. I do not want to marry. I seldom say so, to be disbelieved.'

'You don't feel that marriage would mean a fuller life.'

'I don't want the things it would be full of.' (5)

This is the first half of the dialogue which begins the novel. It is as spare as the talking gets, mostly monosyllabic, terse but repetitive, with no subordinate clauses, decorative epithets or marked rhetoric. Only one out of eight sentences is longer than one line. The absence of names and place isolates and emphasises conversation. It is dialectic, taking the form of direct question or declarative sentence implying question, with an answer to each question. It is dynamic, as the first speaker presses for more than one reason and gets them. The information provided by these first 146 words is considerable: we learn about position, status, professional success, character and relationship; the marriage proposal tells us the gender of the speakers; and we gather that they are used to talking frankly to each other, using almost, though not quite, the same ironic and self-scrutinising language.

The style draws attention to itself. The characters listen carefully, paying full attention to the words they hear, repeating them so that we take notice of the first utterance and the repetitions and expansions. Because the sentences are simple, without clause construction, speech seems to be slowed down. The four exchanges of question and answer contain the repeated, pondered and mutated important words: 'will', 'not', 'last', 'give', 'time', 'reason', 'deep' and 'full'. The exchange of these words develops difference: the man initiates the word, and the woman returns it in a modified form. When she says, 'it may be deep' and 'I don't want the things it would be full of', the first response shows her thought and the second her wit, while we observe in each that what is offered and scrutinised is dead metaphor revived for her argument and for our inspection. It is a little like a Platonic dialogue, a little like the responsive instruments in a string quartet, a little like good tennis. The contrast and interplay of a subversive and a more conventional social attitude are reflected in this rally of ironic styles, and it is interesting that the dead metaphors of depth and fullness, not the re-creative pondering, are used by Hereward, the novelist in the novel. When we look back later, his inferiority of wits and wit in this dialogue illuminates his son Merton's wish not to follow in his famous footsteps.

This art of conversation draws attention to itself, but art is never the only subject, as it is in much postmodernism. This dynamic example is unusual in privacy and intimacy but typical of the novels in making demands on readers, and in rewarding them. Some will enjoy the call for concentration; others find it too austere, too much like hard work, in spite of the wit and humour. But compare that lovers' dialogue with the beginning of so many books by novelists who ask nothing but our time, and reward us only by killing time.

Notes

1. Other examples are Thomas Love Peacock, Henry James and Ronald Firbank.
2. Margaret Jourdain and Ivy Compton-Burnett, 'A Conversation', in *The Art of I. Compton-Burnett*, ed. Burkhart, 21.
3. For *Dolores* I have used the 1971 reprint edited by Burkhart.
4. See Chapter 5 for a full discussion of this subject.
5. Charles Burkhart, *I. Compton-Burnett*, 97–8.

Chapter 3

The Narrative Imagination

Like all good novelists, Compton-Burnett is much possessed by the narratives of everyday life, and her characters remember, anticipate, dream, gossip, confess, and tell the truth. Homer and Mark Twain love liars, Proust concentrates on memory, George Eliot analyses fantasy life, and Compton-Burnett specialises in secrets, rumours, lies, truths and stories told to children.

Her novels are full of inquisitive characters, eavesdropping, hovering outside or inside doors, holding tea-parties or paying calls to gratify what Hope in *Parents and Children* calls a 'devouring' desire to know your neighbours' business. Gossip thrives on secrets, and Compton-Burnett's cupboards are full of skeletons who do what Samuel Butler jokes about: 'If they will only keep to the cupboards . . . It is more serious when the skeletons insist on answering the hall-door bell, button-holing everyone who comes to the house, and telling them all about it.'[1] She developed stylised methods of conveying scandal and rumour: hot news of marriages, deaths, illegitimate children and inheritances is carried round the houses at top speed by tradesmen and servants.

Here conversation is the medium of gossip, comic and seriously self-analytic. The significant exchange of words can be destructive, as it is in *A House and Its Head*, a novel with dark secrets at its heart – the infant Richard Edgeworth was not fathered by his mother's husband, and died of gas-poisoning in mysterious circumstances. An intricate chain of false rumours is started by his half-sister, Sibyl Edgeworth, who arranges his murder to get his inheritance. She tells her husband she suspects her father and his third wife, and when he is dismissive makes him promise he 'won't breathe a syllable', but confides in Dulcia Bode, waiting with her do-gooder companion, Beatrice, to welcome Sibyl and Grant after their wedding journey. Sibyl affects 'a low, half weeping tone' – 'Dulcia

. . . people always say strange things, when something happens, don't they?' (224–6) – then repeats a rumour about Grant fathering the child. Dulcia tells her to forget it and go on with her life, but she insists that Duncan and Cassie are guilty, eventually coming to the point:

'I can't drive it out of my mind; it keeps coming back; a picture keeps coming up of Cassie, creeping up to Richard's bed; with Father behind her, creeping too; and both with a look that says he is not their own, and must yield to another child who will be hers and his. It can't mean anything? It can't mean that Father and Cassie wished that he would die? It can't mean Father did? It is not true that people who have had a shock, have second-sight, is it?' (227)

Sibyl is imagined as a skilful story-teller, pace slow, dramatis personae particularised, imagery vivid, speech disturbed and wild. Grant joins them and she switches to concerned questioning: 'Grant, did Richard suffer? I have not dared to ask,' and 'Would there have been a moment, when he was conscious of something, and could not overcome it? He was so helpless' (227). Her tone of 'acute misery and grief' is faked but her ignorance genuine, since she arranged but did not witness the murder. Dulcia advises Grant that she needs sleep, and leaves to pick up where Sibyl left off, becoming the teller of the tale with Beatrice as eager listener.

There is a long conversation showing Compton-Burnett's narrative imagination at its most subtly devastating as it deals with two of her favourite subjects, secrets and gossip. Dulcia steps out of her comic function to spread the malicious rumour about Richard's death and in doing so changes her style. Her idiolect is marked by platitude, cliché and hearty slang but as gossip she affects silence and discretion, using a teasing narrative retardation which stirs curiosity and builds to a climax, stopping just before her revelation. She has the perfect listener in Beatrice, another extrovert do-gooder, and unusually for her, she takes her time, insisting that she cannot repeat 'the truth':

'Sibyl is very much affected by the shock . . . I am not at liberty to divulge the truth, but no one would believe it, who had not her confidence.'
'I suppose it is natural.'
'It is not natural: it is morbid and strange. As I said, I should not have believed it.'
'I should, you know,' said Beatrice, in a frank tone. 'I saw she was over-wrought, in all the ways that do not go into words.'

'You have no suspicion, happily for your peace. And it did go into words, unhappily for mine.'

'I have not much peace on her account, I confess.'

'You would have none, if you knew.'

'I do not know specifically, of course; but I have a shrewd suspicion.'

'No, dear; your suspicion may be shrewd; but you are not on the nail here. No. And I am glad you are not.'

'Can I help you in the place you are in?'

'No, I am not going to reveal it. I must be strong. I must not be led into betraying a trust, by such insinuating offers.'

'I did not suggest you should reveal it.'

'Not specifically, of course,' said Dulcia, smiling over the phrase. 'But there does lurk a tiny hope of revelation in such approach.' (228)

Dulcia is not only going slowly but dwelling with uncharacteristic subtlety on her own words and those of Beatrice. There is something sinister in the change of style, her usual impetuous and thoughtless speed giving way to a reflective mode and pace as she entices her susceptible listener to believe the false rumour about Duncan and Cassie, started in her own susceptible mind by Sibyl. Instead of bouncing from one strong dead metaphor to another in her usual style, she pauses, thinks, repeats words thoughtfully, to rouse Beatrice's attention and make her slow down to take in the hints. The conversation shifts to the introspective concern with word and phrase shown by more thoughtful and truthful characters, not so much in a change of character as a shift from concentration on words to concentration on narrative – the tone and pace of slander, the slowed, hushed voices of gossips whispering behind their hands. The dialogue develops the two women's complicity, and, as tension builds, concludes with Dulcia's intention to confide her secret. Because teller and listener are Christians, the concluding vow seems blasphemous:

'It is unlike me to keep anything from you; but I am not my own mistress here.'

'You should have been enough so, to avoid mention of it.'

'I should. It is mean to stimulate curiosity, without the power of gratifying it.'

'I am not conscious of more curiosity than you make a point of exciting. A little is due to your effort, isn't it? But has it not been effort in a wrong cause?' Beatrice smiled and swung her umbrella.

'Darling, I won't torment you any more . . .'

'Do not tell me anything you feel you should not.'

'I have got to the stage of feeling I positively should. Your patience and

forbearance reveal you as a suitable repository for my confidence. And it
is to be a confidence, utter, unbreakable, eternal, so help us God.' (228–9)

It is a clever conclusion: the novelist is narrating cleverly enough to
stop short just before the teller comes out with the story – which we
never hear. Both women speak more thoughtfully and quietly than usual,
Dulcia without what she calls her 'unwary words', Beatrice without her
smug piety, because they are talking scandal, Dulcia tantalising, Beatrice
eager and expectant. There is the suggestive sibilance of whispering: 'specifically, of course . . . shrewd suspicion', 'positively should', 'patience
and forbearance . . . suitable repository' and 'so help us'. It is the poetry
of evil tongues.

It gathers momentum between chapters. At a charitable 'Dorcas'
meeting in the next chapter, Dulcia pretends to support the guiltless
Edgeworths: 'They will come out with their faces turned to the music,
if I know them . . .' Mr Burtenshaw asks, 'Why, is there any music for
them to face?' She answers, 'The hardest music of all, the music of
slandering tongues,' but he 'adjures' her to speak plainly: 'I can't do
with whispering and clapping of hands to mouths. I only imagine things
worse than the truth.' His daughter, Rosamond, informed by Beatrice
in that space between the last chapter and this, informs everyone, 'They
have already been imagined.' Her father tells her to speak plainly but
Beatrice, like Dulcia sworn to secrecy, gets in first, saying, 'in a low
tone', 'I think there is some rumour about Mr and Mrs Edgeworth's
causing the death of the child' (230). Rumour spreads and swells, in a
master-class on the *mauvaise langue* as brilliant and elaborate as Virgil's
Fama[2] and Sheridan's *School for Scandal*.

Compton-Burnett likes to offer the narrative contrast of lies with
truth, and Dulcia and her gossips meet their match in Gretchen Jekyll,
who arrives in time to observe Dulcia taking a vote on the subject of
the Edgeworths' guilt:

'So your suspicions have made you a great game!' said a voice at the
door, as Gretchen entered with her son.
There was silence.
'I suppose we could hear a pin drop,' muttered Fabian . . .
'We did not see you, dear Mrs Jekyll,' said Dulcia.
'A difficult and thankless task, the pin,' said Fabian.
'It was I who saw you.'
'Then you saw us bearing witness to our belief in your daughter and
her husband.'

'You found it noble in yourselves to acquit your friends of what you put on to them.' (232)

When Dulcia tries to make light of the rumours by imaging them as a 'cloud of dust' (233) and 'The merest, lightest gossip, blown away like a piece of thistledown', Gretchen shows that two can play with metaphor: 'Thistledown in dispersing goes a good many ways' and 'Thistledown is in the air . . . It does hang about' (234–5). One of Compton-Burnett's great truth-tellers, Gretchen is the *dea ex machina*, who, a little later, carries out a skilful detective enterprise, testing the suspect, making deductions and exposing the criminal.

Slander usually involves a lie, as it does in Sibyl's story, and lying is another form of narrative dramatised with scathing critique, tolerance and sympathy. It is treated comically in *Pastors and Masters*, where everybody lies: Mr Merry is employed to lie to parents about the children; Nicholas Herrick and Richard Bumpus lie about writing their novels, one filched and the other a revision of an old one; and the intelligent Emily Herrick lies benignly to everyone except her best friend, using her knowledge and judgement to protect her weak, dishonest brother. The plot and action of *Brothers and Sisters* is based on two serious lies, Andrew Stace's lie about the paternity of Christian and Sophia Stace's tacit lie – kept up over many years – about what she believes to be her father's will in a locked drawer. The destructive liars are almost always found out, though Anna Donne in *Elders and Betters* is a chilling exception.

Ninian in *The Mighty and Their Fall* is a bad liar, unscrupulous, blatant, unconvincing and naïve. His dying brother, Ransom, asks him to destroy one will and keep the other, and finds, as he expected, that Ninian has preserved the one in his own favour. Ninian is flustered:

'Now what of the wills? Earlier and later! Later and earlier! You have found another and been puzzled by it.'

'I have found this one. The one you should have destroyed. I forced myself to reach the chest. I had a feeling that I should do so. And it was a sound one.'

'You mistrusted me and my preoccupations? Then why did you give me such a charge?'

'No one would be inattentive in a matter like this.'

'Well, did I make a muddle?' said Ninian, drawing in his brows. 'Is this the will from the chest or another one?'

'You know there is no other.' (125)

And a little later:

Ninian remained with his eyes contracted on the will.
'There is nothing amiss with your sight. It is the kind that is good for reading. And you found it good.'
'Then there is something amiss with *me*,' said Ninian lightly, 'There must be, if you say the truth. I must have had a fit of mental blankness . . .' (126)

Ninian's pretence that he is short-sighted, and his light reply, are examples of Compton-Burnett's rare and skilful use of stage direction. The reader watches Ninian keep up his threadbare lie, in dramatically ironic awareness, but in *The Present and the Past* Cassius discusses his attempt at suicide in a long, emotionally varied performance; the reader is taken in, and shocked with the family when his lying is accidentally exposed. But many liars are understood and excused. In *Daughters and Sons*, the children need to lie to their tyrannical grandmother, and as she pries, 'Was there some exciting letter?' (114), they say it was just an argument and she knows they are lying. She asks Edith, the new governess, 'in her ruthless manner', 'Do you like lies?' to be told, 'No, I like to know the exact truth about the smallest thing. It is the result of a narrow life' (115). A little later, Edith asks, 'What about that lie you told to your grandmother? I see a lie is a little daily event' and offers to help their deception about France's secret career as a novelist (118). In *Parents and Children*, the children are complicit in keeping truths from their mother: 'Oh, just tell a fib,' says Isabel to her sister when she wants to avoid a fuss (162), and James lies almost every day about being too ill to go to school, and reading adult books. But these lies are nothing compared with those told by Ridley Cranmer, who almost lies his way into bigamy, and by Sir Jesse Sullivan who tells his illegitimate children that he is childless.

In *More Women than Men*, Josephine Napier lies about everything, suppressing and inventing facts. She always lies about her nephew, Gabriel, whose marriage she does her jealous best to ignore:

'Well, I have not lost Gabriel,' said Josephine in an almost comfortable tone. 'I must take myself to task, and remind myself how much I have in the concentration of his feeling; and not fret about his having to tear himself away in the flesh. But poor boy! His face at parting does come back to me; it will. I am not one to make a fuss about nothing; but this is not quite nothing.' (140)

And:

> 'Oh, I have had it all,' said Josephine, almost airily. 'How hard it is to throw oneself into a new life, when the old is tugging from the past—that was the word, tugging; not elegant, is it?—and how long it will seem before the upheaval is over . . .' (141)

The plausible lies are invented by a novelist, here using her powers of solid specification and close scrutiny of lexis. When there are stage directions, they are chosen with care; those scrupulous 'almosts' register Josephine's careful attention to tone.

Compton-Burnett is good on the dishonesties of everyday life, the white lies we tell for self-aggrandisement or to improve a story. In *Manservant and Maidservant*, Bullivant lies about telling a lie. Asked if he heaped coal on the fire, he says no; when told someone saw him, he says it slipped his mind; and then he lies to the other servants about the episode, saying he had confessed immediately to building up the fire. Like other unctuous manservants in the novels, he habitually indulges in self-flattering stories about his master's attachment to him. In the same novel, Miss Buchanan, the shopkeeper, grudgingly lets Gertrude Doubleday shelter from the rain and she tells a pointless lie which transforms the incident into a self-flattering special invitation. Miss Buchanan herself provides a moral contrast: she is a sympathetic liar, highly motivated and as honest as possible, avoiding the direct lie about her illiteracy, and intelligently contriving excuses and evasions.

Another self-aggrandising story, not false in fact but false in feeling, comes in *A Family and a Fortune*, when Matty tells dishonest stories that are exaggerations, elbowing out other speakers in attempts to engross an unimpressed audience. She is the egocentric story-teller, her favourite subject herself when young and attractive, here combining boasts about her surface charm and her depth:

> 'I am a person who lives rather in the deeps . . . But I have a surface self to show to my niece and nephews, so that I need not take them down too far with me. I have a deal to tell them of the time when I was as young as they, and things were different and yet the same, in that strange way things have. Yes, there are stories awaiting you of Aunt Matty in her heyday, when the world was young, or seemed to keep itself young for her, as things did somehow adapt themselves for her in those days. Now there is quite a lot for Aunt Matty to talk about herself. But you asked her, didn't you?' Matty looked about in a bright, conscious way and tapped her knee. (81–2)

On a later visit, she turns the talk from Dudley's fortune to her own story:

> Matty at once addressed the group as if to forestall any other speaker.
>
> 'Now I must tell you of something which happened to me when I was young, something which this occasion in your lives brings back to me. I too might have been left a fortune. When we are young, things are active or would be if we let them, or so it was in my youth. Well, a man was in love with me or said he was; and I could see it for myself, so I cannot leave it out; and I refused him – well, we won't dwell on that . . .' (125)

After the story ends with the suitor's death and Matty's 'narrow escape from a fortune', Miss Griffin takes the subject back to Dudley, 'Was that a large fortune, too?', to be snubbed: 'It was large enough to call one. That is all that matters for the story.' She holds centre-stage for a moment. Her niece, Justine, wishes there had been no heirs and Matty might have had a better life but, too vain to accept sympathy, she says, 'an easier later chapter, dear'; she has no regrets because she has lived up 'to the best' that was in her. This sentimental reminiscence is egocentric and self-flattering, like Josephine Napier's plausible boasts and lies, but with a twist: Matty's story 'had a note of truth which no one credited' (126).

In a different class is the narrator–nursery-maid, Mullet, in *Parents and Children*, who tells the children a gripping serial about her fall from wealth and rank:

> 'Yes, I will give you the last chapter of my childhood . . . I was often by myself for hours, as I had no equal in the house, and I preferred my own company to that of inferiors. Well, there I was sitting, in my shabby, velvet dress, swinging my feet in their shabby, velvet shoes; my things were good when they came, but I was really rather neglected; and there came a ring at the bell, and my father was in the house. "And what is this?" he said, when he had hastened to my place of refuge. "How comes it that I find my daughter alone and unattended?"' (77–8)

An ironic commentary draws attention to the skill with which the story-teller parries questions, and her relief when truth and fiction chance to coincide: 'You told us you had a maid of your own'; '"My last nurse was on the way to a maid. But I was quite without one on that day when my father came home; absolutely without," said Mullet, with evident attention to accuracy'; and 'Sometimes I can hardly

believe myself in my own early life' (79). Her tall stories are set-piece
monologues which the children's credulous or sceptical responses nicely
assimilate: Mullet says she owes her 'being' to her father and Honor
suggests that it may be the other way round (204). Unlike Odysseus
and Huckleberry Finn, Mullet does not find credulous listeners, and she
is not exposed by Honor's sly aside. Faulty constructions and peculiar
lexis play a part in the comedy of this social narrative, and when Honor
corrects Mullet's mispronunciation of 'horizon' (203), the story-teller
refers plausibly to her neglected education, which is part of the story.
In spite of the obvious motive of class envy or aspiration, one of the
fascinations of the nursery-maid's wild fantasies is their freedom and
redundancy. Odysseus and Huck start lying in order to survive, improv-
ing technique and forming a habit, but Mullet always invents for the
joy of inventing, as a skilled professional placed centre-stage – but never
for long – by an appreciative creator who knows what it is to love one's
creation.

Compton-Burnett's people often lie to keep their secrets, and there
are secrets at the heart of most of the novels. In *Pastors and Masters*,
Herrick lies to keep the secret of his plagiarism, and Bumpus to keep the
secret about his pretence that he destroyed his first novel for romantic
reasons. Only William and Emily see the truths behind the lies, but
William keeps silence and Emily confides in Theresa, needing to tell the
truth to someone. Her truth-telling compromises her, and shows her
deliberated conventional acquiescence in social norms, as she succumbs
to the ironist's temptation – which is cynicism.

There is one strikingly prominent group of truth-tellers – the children.
They are endowed with simple candour, a devastating lack of tact, and
an ignorance of polite norms which frees them to speak – like Paul in
Dombey and Son asking his capitalist father about money – from a
crystalline, innocent clear-sightedness. In *Manservant and Maidservant*,
Avery Lamb surprises us by defending the good side of his father Horace,
who has terribly neglected and frightened him. In *The Present and the
Past*, the children of Cassius Clare, who knows himself so slenderly,
insist on telling the whole truth and nothing but the truth, offending their
dishonest father and delighting their truth-telling mother and stepmother.
The children speak surprisingly well of him after his death, not because
they follow the maxim of speaking no evil of the dead but because his
death makes them see his life as a whole, as a completed story.

The exceptional children who do lie have been contaminated by the
adult world, like the fantasists Julius and Dora in *Elders and Betters*,

daunted but perhaps also over-influenced by their deeply religious mother, or Clemence and Sefton in *Two Worlds and Their Ways*, who cheat and lie because they are driven by their parents' great expectations. Her pure truth-telling children articulate and emphasise Compton-Burnett's concern with social contingency; they are innocents who have not yet been exposed to our powerful cultures of lying.

Notes

1. Samuel Butler, *Samuel Butler's Notebooks*, 195.
2. Virgil, *The Aeneid*.

Chapter 4

Languages of Feeling

How does Compton-Burnett express strong emotion and passion? I know some readers find her too cold in the narration and impersonation of feeling, and there is certainly a marked difference between her affective forms and those of most other novelists – for instance, Richardson, Austen, George Eliot, Henry James, and modernists like Joyce, Lawrence and Beckett – who offer access to the emotional life of characters, and sometimes represent narrators with sympathetic feelings about their fictions and the life outside fiction. Compton-Burnett usually presents exterior behaviour and speech in detached narration, very seldom showing characters in solitude or with one other person. Her stories are social and public, dealing with surfaces and rarely imaging or dramatising personal depths. But there are a few moments of strong feeling or passion, presented in narration, image or description, impressively brief and understated. They are unusual in fiction in never, or hardly ever, expressing sexual or romantic passion; such passions are not excluded but they are implied and never, or hardly ever, stated. She hardly ever invites the reader to identify or sympathise with the feelings of her characters.[1]

Sophia, the central character in *Brothers and Sisters* (1929), Compton-Burnett's first fully accomplished novel, shows an intensity of grief and love, and, though its form of expression is not new, the implications are complex. Compton-Burnett is clearly interested in the question of emotional sincerity and several of her characters affect feeling, like Josephine Napier in *More Women than Men* or Hetta Ponsonby in *Daughters and Sons*. In Sophia's case, however, the expression of strong feeling is neither insincere nor affected:

'Miss Patmore,' said Sophia, pausing white and tense before her; 'you have been with me through all my time of happiness. You were with me at the hour of my romance. You have watched my feeling for my husband grow with my growth, with every day of the twenty-seven years we have gone our way together. Now it is threatened, Miss Patmore, our love and our life with each other. It is not safe any longer. Christian is ill; his heart is not right. He is a sick man, my husband. He has told me as he promised he would. How thankful I am that I made him give me that word! It is the illness that Mrs Lang had, his mother. There is this great cloud come over us!'

Sophia, in her extreme moments, when she suffered more than most, never ceased to listen to herself. (105–6)

This is telling and showing, on the part of both author and character: eager to make sure we do not misread, the narrator says Sophia 'suffered more than most', and more discreetly, that she is 'white and tense', but shows her awareness of her feelings as she claims the right to confide them. Her emotional speech to the old nurse and housekeeper, whom she trusts, is necessary – driven by feeling, presented formally in conspicuous repetition, exclamation, and the metaphor of 'a great cloud', eloquent explanation as well as heartfelt appeal. The character recalls the past, deliberately choosing a listener who shares it and will understand her grief because she has witnessed her love. The novelist mediates the expression of love, grief and fear through a carefully reasoned act of confidence, in which we may hear the character listening to herself.

Like E. M. Forster, Compton-Burnett knows that unpleasant and imperfect people are capable of strong feeling. Never a sympathetic character, Sophia is at her most selfish, self-indulgent and insensitive when, ten months after Christian's death, she is found expressing intense grief, engrossing and impeding her children's lives. She complains because they are not back from a country walk:

'Oh, no one knows what people go through, when they have such a temperament as I have,' said Sophia, sitting down. 'No one knows what I imagine, what pictures I call up, what scenes I live through with my dear ones, when they are away from my care. For the one death my husband died, I died for him thirty times.' (161)

Her lamentation comes across again as both sincere and highly self-conscious, conspicuously repeating the figure of *occupatio*, 'no one knows', and hyperbole, 'I died for him thirty times'. But when she goes on to tell her old confidante that she has worries about her own health – which prove well founded – we see the strong emotion, and also the awareness – 'I know' – expressed in a looser, more colloquial style – 'Well, now' and 'you know':

> 'Well, now, I have something else to bring down on you, Miss Patmore. My children are safe; so I can turn my attention to myself, to my poor old self. I must come second to them; I know; I do come after them in my own thoughts. Well, you know, Miss Patmore, I don't think I am well.' Sophia's voice broke and she went on, weeping. 'I don't think my health is what it ought to be. I am sure it is not . . . I feel, if I am to find that anything serious is amiss with me, that I cannot go on. I have borne enough.' (161–2)

The sincerity of self-conscious performance – that listening to self – is implicitly discussed again when she is nearing death:

> The time was one of relief and surprise to those who served. Sophia, who had never brooked a challenge to her will, seemed to bow to the extinction of herself. Her nature protected itself, and in the moods when she greatly wished to live, she felt she would not die. It was not Sophia's personality that was diseased. Moreover, did she always so fiercely wish to live? Had life been so sweet to Sophia? More was learnt of her in her numbered days. In her thousand asseverations, that life could offer no more to her, had there been the touch of truth? Was there truth at the bottom of Sophia? (191)

This is a formal narrative, which is a conclusion but inconclusive enough to raise questions; the narrator is not omniscient. The affective form of the whole book has been determined by the dramatised trajectory of Sophia's emotions, which now ends, but at this point the author looks back and re-opens the story in a free, indirect style, joining viewpoints of community and narrator: 'There had seldom been such feeling in Moreton Edge as was stirred by the death of Sophia Stace. Sophia's spirit, with its strength, and the strength of its weakness, had taken hold on the place of her birth, and tore up the soil when it went' (208). It is an obituary composed of balanced assessment and sudden impassioned metaphor. Fairly judged and summed up, Sophia is the first of Compton-Burnett's strong, unpleasant characters to occupy the centre of the novel, dominating readers as well as other characters, subverting those conventional and admirable heroes and heroines with whom we love to identify.

The sympathetic Charlotte Lamb in *Manservant and Maidservant* makes an impassioned reproach and complaint to her husband, who has changed his mean and tyrannical ways after discovering that she and his cousin Mortimer had planned to leave and take the children:

> 'We will not have a great and unusual silence. Mortimer and I could not suffer the things in this house; we were at the end of our power to suffer. We could let helpless children suffer no longer, after seeing them do so all their lives . . . But I have come home to find this difference, this difference that there might always have been. If you had been like this always, Horace! If you had lived this life from the first! This is proof that you could have done so, that you could have made the hard path easy. It does not show the past in a better light. But for the moment our case is gone . . . The future is in your hands, and you have the power to hold it. But the past is my tragedy and your fault. You must not be a martyr. You must not put me to a longer martyrdom.' (145)

The speech is criticised by Burkhart as 'strident and theatrical', an example of a 'kind of language reserved for scenes of high emotion', and an 'odd, even jarring' contrast with 'the general texture of wit', though he compares it with the 'bombast' of Corneille, and admits that such passages are rare and 'have a certain appeal'.[2] It is markedly rhetorical, like some of Sophia's speeches, with balance, repetition, biblical echo and exclamations, and a few banalities or dead metaphors, but it is thoughtful, self-analytic and psychologically apt. It is a speech made with an effort – she clenches her hands in preparation – and speech after long silence. Charlotte is flouting the formidable Horace, who enters the room with his aunt 'as though bringing a witness', and says they will not speak of 'the thing' that is between them. When he admits that she speaks 'well', she retorts: 'It is the result of my not having spoken before.'

Dudley Gaveston in *A Family and a Fortune* is a sympathetic, unheroic and often isolated character, to whose inner life and feeling we are given more than the usual access. Towards the end of the novel, he leaves the home where he is no longer at home and befriends Miss Griffin, who has been callously turned out on a cold night by her employer, Matty:

> Dudley put his arm about her, and walked on, leading her with him. She went without a word, taking her only course and trusting to his aid. Her short, quick, unequal steps, the steps of someone used to being on her feet, but not to walking out of doors, made no attempt to keep time or pace, and he saw with a pang how she might try the nerves of anyone in daily contact. The pang drove him on as if in defiance of its warning. (237–8)

His pity is stirred by proximity and fellow-feeling, with a touch of condescension to the pitied and danger to the one who pities, but the feeling is too strong to be restrained by common sense and Dudley impetuously proposes marriage, to be prudently turned down. His companion is thinking, and imagining: '"Oh, no, no! . . . What a thing it would be. Of course not. We could not alter it when it was done and of course you would want to." Her voice was sympathetic, as if her words hardly concerned herself' (238). Miss Griffin too has her particularised trajectory of feeling, and this is a significant moment, when, in spite of her distress and need, her intelligence works for them both, also preserving her from self-abasement.

After he finds her shelter with a neighbour, his mood changes, and he recovers a tranquillity and self-possession he has not felt since he lost his beloved fiancée to his more deeply beloved brother. This is one of the rare narrated interiorisations, and a scene of solitude:

> He slept as he had not slept since his brother's engagement, the sense of suspense and waiting leaving him at last. He found that his mind and emotions were cleared, and that his feeling for Edgar had taken its own place. He had been lost in the tumult of his own life, and the hour passed in another's had done its work. Edgar stood in his heart above any other. (239)

The particularised feelings are self-generative, always on the move. Dudley's return to what George Eliot calls 'our persistent self'[3] is not simple, and the passage continues, 'The knowledge brought the relief of simplified emotion, but fed his anger with his brother, and confirmed his resolution to remain out of his life' (239). The long episode takes us inside the character, with a commentary kept close to his inner movements of thought and feeling. We are invited to observe and understand, in plain, simple language, and without the demand for excitement or empathy made by the narrator's emotionally charged imagery in *Middlemarch*. Burkhart tells us that *A Family and a Fortune* is 'about money', but it is also about the long, irreplaceable love of siblings, wonderfully dramatised in Sophocles' *Antigone*.

Brotherly love often occurs in the novels, but the passion which seems to recur most often is one the novelist had never felt – mother-love. It is often combined with grief, caused by deprivation and death, and first appears in the second novel, *Pastors and Masters* (1925), where the feeling is dramatically presented in one look and one sentence, and summed up in one adverb. Theresa Fletcher, one of the two rational women (and three rational people) in the novel, is brought to think of her dead sons during a polite dinner-party conversation. A fellow-guest says to Theresa's husband, 'You have no children, have you?' He replies, 'Not living . . . We have had two sons,' and there follows a stage direction describing the felt silence as 'Theresa gazed fiercely in front of her' (86). It is almost certainly Theresa and not her husband who then says, 'Yes, there is not much good in rearing up children, when they are to be killed off one by one' – one of many speeches in the novels which we may have to read more than once in order to identify the speaker (86). Theresa is described by the embarrassed fellow-guest as 'very sensitive' (86).

The adjective 'fierce' was used in the first summary description of Theresa – 'a large old woman, with fierce eyes looking out between a massive brow and chin' (29) – and if we recall or re-read this, the repetition at the dinner-party confirms the grief as long, settled and dominant. The novel is one of the few to be set in the post-war period, and the words 'killed off' and 'one by one' indicate war casualties. Compton-Burnett's two much-loved brothers died during the war, one of influenza and the other in the Battle of the Somme, so she did not have to imagine the waste and loss of war, and here represents it briefly in the bereavement of a long-grieving, bitter mother. *Pastors and Masters* is like Virginia Woolf's *Mrs Dalloway* in telling a story which obliquely or gradually reveals its concern with the aftermath of war, and this strong moment of feeling is part of the novel's understatement.

In *Parents and Children* (1941), there is another mother whose children have died – we are not told how or when – and who is a grandmother. Her ruling passion is described when she is first introduced, and echoes the key word used for Theresa's bitter sorrow: 'Regan[4] was a woman who only loved her family. She loved her husband deeply, her children fiercely' (15). The 'fiercely' is explained when her granddaughter Luce says, 'Your children must have always found you a refuge from the censorious world,' and we are told, 'Regan's face worked at mention of her children, two of whom were dead' (17). The three generations are at lunch as they discuss the voyage to be taken by Regan's son Fulbert. Her grandson Graham glances at her, 'in imagination of her feeling', and she shows that feeling: 'I shall not live six months many more times' (21). Other feelings about the departure come up: Fulbert states, 'Those who show the least, feel the most,' and Regan says, '"That is not the line to take with me" . . . with smiling reference to her swift emotions' (23). A little later, her husband, Jesse, breaks into song, 'in muffled reminiscent tones, which seemed at once to croon with sentiment and throb with experience':

> He glanced at the portraits of his dead son and daughter, as if his emotion prepared the way for recalling them; and sang on, as though the possession of life overcame all else.
>
> His wife followed his look and his thought, though her eyes were not on him. She would have given her life for her children's, and knew he would have done this for nothing at all, and accepted and supported his feeling. (24)

The narrator is contrasting two responses, and Jesse's ruthless love of life, of which we hear more later in the story, gives definition to the commonplace about giving your life for your child; we see what it means by seeing what it means not to feel such self-sacrificial love, and seeing it, and seeing Regan's loving tolerance, prevents us from feeling that her maternal passion is too extreme or self-indulgent. Compton-Burnett is using two ways of presenting this passion, dramatising it in the talk about Fulbert's trip, then narrating it in the comparison with Jesse – though in precise and particular terms.

Regan with her surviving child and Theresa with her dead children are both fierce in their mother-love, and though the use of 'fierce' and 'fiercely' is narrative and not dramatic, telling not showing, the epithets are strong and surprising, words used to describe anger or aggression, not grief or sorrow. The implication is that these women resent their loss, and are fierce against fate. Compton-Burnett is describing an expression, not a feeling, tacitly agreeing with D. H. Lawrence, who believed that to name or describe emotion is to simplify, separate, classify, single out and falsify.[5] To use the word 'fierce' of these grieving women is truthful, not claiming to go beyond or behind behaviour, while emphasising the complexity of the affective life.

The two characters are unlike as well as alike in their passion. Theresa only speaks of it once and gives her detached but not uncaring attention to the outside world and her friendship with Emily Herrick, whose rationality she shares, while Regan frequently refers to her own strong maternal feeling, with ease, irony and even humour. Theresa has no descendants, and plays little part in the short novel, but Regan is a prominent figure, and her ruling passion takes several forms. Later in the story, she thinks that Fulbert is dead and she is left childless, and when later still she learns he may be alive, she passionately seizes the hope and immediately rushes off to find him, recalling for us that 'fierce' which introduced her grief and devotion. Her motherliness extends to her grandchildren, most sensitively in a story she tells three-year-old Nevill when his father has returned – to surprise reader and characters. Nevill brings her a nest, and she spontaneously seizes the moment:

'A bird's nest,' he said. 'Where the little birds used to live.'
  'What will they do without their home?'
  'All fly away,' said Nevill.
  'The little birds had a father and mother bird,' said Regan, guiding his head towards Fulbert. 'And the father bird has come back to the nest.'
  Nevill cast his eyes about in search of this visitor, and dropped them to the nest, in case Regan's words might be true.
  'Where?' he said, bringing them back to her face.
  'Look and see,' said Regan, turning his head again in the right direction.
  'Outside,' said Nevill, as some sparrows chirped by the window, 'He has come back. Hark!' (274–5)

The novelist is too tactful to show Nevill making the connection; his father makes the move, and the child is soon whimpering and laughing in his arms. Regan's warm, sensitive touch, actual and metaphorical, is shown in the good, imaginative parenting her daughter-in-law cannot manage. She shows – and is shown by – a narrative poetry her author rarely offers, and does so here in a story within the story, which can risk simple fancy and allegory because it is told to a very young child. Regan's mother-love not only is a compelling feeling that animates her character, but also is compared and contrasted with other kinds of parental affection to emphasise the book's main theme, and influences the course of the plot.

In *A God and His Gifts*, the complexity of a strong feeling is shown by the use of one sentence spoken by Hetty, a character who is not central like Sophia and Regan but has been prominent and fallen into the background. Her expressive speech avoids the naming which cannot be truthful or accurate; like the adjective 'fierce' and the adverb 'fiercely', it is a brief signifier, a simile used to express a deep mother-love. This time, the feeling is sad rather than fierce. Hetty, the mother of two children, Henry and Maud, is deprived of her son, who is illegitimate; he is adopted by his father, her ex-lover and father-in-law, Hereward, the god of the title, and their true relationship is, for a long time, a secret. She often sees Henry but he does not know her as his mother and there is no doubt about her bitter mother-love and painful deprivation.

On one occasion, she and her husband, Merton, Hereward's son, are visiting Henry in his nursery. Hetty looks at him sitting on his grandmother's knee, Merton mentions Maud, and Hetty says: 'They both change with every day like flowers' (97). It is a dramatic moment, in which the novelist imagines, utters and images the mother's private love, delight, grief and loss, which can only be expressed indirectly, through the brilliantly abstract and sensuous simile of the brief, bright life of flowers.[6] The image wryly implies a fond observation this mother cannot make every day but can infer from watching the other child, the one she may acknowledge and hold in love.

We return to the mother's gaze in the last chapter, when the novel, which plays with secret family relationships and the danger of incest, ends with an apparently far from subtle in-joke about Hetty's children. Sir Michael, the grandfather, has just died, and Merton and Hetty are paying a formal visit to the family house. Hereward, the heir, more godly than ever, has succeeded to title and estate, and Merton, who now knows the secret of Henry's paternity, looks gloomily to the future and fears that 'The truth . . . may bear on coming lives' (171). Hetty hears Maud and her nurse in the hall, says 'It is time to go,' and we are told that, 'as always', she 'had been watching Henry' (171).

Maud comes in, and the children's egotism is comically portrayed as they quarrel over a pencil and then apply themselves to their separate drawings. Hetty is ignored by Henry, though the novelist does not draw attention to his response, as in an earlier scene, when he calls her 'sister Hetty' . . . 'in a tone of quotation' after her eyes follow him and she asks him to say goodnight to her (98). At the end, she asks Maud, 'Don't you want to see Henry's picture?' (172). There is more dark talk from Merton: 'He will have to grow up and marry . . .' Henry murmurs, 'Marry', and, asked jokingly by Hereward, 'Whom would you like to have?', answers 'Dear little Maud' (173). The scene is crowded with many feelings and many characters. Hetty says very little and is never the centre of attention, so we may not remark the vast affective distance between the neat, clinching, ironic last line and the tender pity of that earlier rare, poetic image. But if we are good enough readers of the novels to be alerted by the brief repetition of that maternal gaze, the incest joke at the end will strike us as less amusing.

Strong feeling is sometimes shown even more reticently. There is a moment on the last page of *Darkness and Day* when, after Mrs Spruce, the cook, has been rudely reminded of her secret past, she gets out a photograph of herself as a young woman with her baby, and compares its image with the reflection in her mirror.

Mrs Spruce pushed back her hair to bring her hand across her face, and went upstairs with a flush spreading over it. She sat down on her bed to grasp and confront her knowledge. She had faced other things in her life, and hardly shrunk from the effort. Then she went to a chest and took out a photograph, and stood with her eyes upon it . . .

She held it by her face before the glass, tracing the changes of the years. Then she restored it to its place, and went downstairs with an air at once resigned and resolute. (254)

Mrs Spruce is a sympathetic character but we are not explicitly invited to admire or pity her. The scene is charged with complex feeling, and we follow its narrative slowly, closely, perhaps re-reading to take it all in. The first sentence describes the woman's involuntary physical response to what she has just heard, which is not felt until she is alone. The second briefly records the need to 'grasp', before facing, the experience of hearing her own story, and is brought up to date with the news of her old lover's death. The third is a curt, condensed and elliptical retrospect of character and event, marked by that significant 'hardly' in 'hardly shrunk from the effort'. The fifth images the life-story as she deliberately stages and scans it, as we see her deciding to put together, to face, then facing, the two faces of youth and age. The last sentence, which shows feeling as well as describing it, marks a wry acceptance of things as they are. The short scene is packed with action, external and internal, described and implied; its stillness and movement are eloquent.[7]

The novelist's forms and figures of feeling animate and develop complex characters like Sophia, Regan and Dudley, and bring apparently marginal characters like Theresa, Hetty and Mrs Spruce into the centre of action, to startle us by moving from surface to depths.

Notes

1. There are exceptions. Horace terrifies his son: '"No rubbish is to be bought. I put my foot down there." He made the actual movement, and Avery unconsciously copied it, as he stood with his eyes upon him.' Horace says the worst selfishness is extravagance, 'to be extirpated, rooted out, by whatever method is the soundest', and Avery says, '"It is a dreadful thing," with his eyes on Horace's face.' His terror is shown by look, movement and five words (*Manservant and Maidservant*, 42–4).

2. Charles Burkhart cites Angus Wilson's criticism of Compton-Burnett's 'purple passages' in support of the judgement: *I. Compton-Burnett*, 38–9.

3. *Middlemarch*, Chapter 15.
4. The name is explained by Regan's father's ignorance of *King Lear* and accepted by her as a name which must have existed before Shakespeare used it.
5. 'The Novel and the Feelings', in *Phoenix: The Posthumous Papers of D. H. Lawrence*, 755–60.
6. Compton-Burnett loved flowers.
7. I have discussed this scene more fully, and in the context of the whole novel, in Chapter 10, repeating the quoted passage and some of the brief discussion in this chapter.

Chapter 5

Creatures and Conditions

In Henry James's 'The Lesson of Balzac', he praises the predecessor, whose broad-ranging, extrovert fiction was so different from his own, for presenting 'the complicated human creature or human condition'.[1] I think that 'or' identifies creature with conditions, James and Balzac perceiving that we are shaped by contingencies of class, gender, milieu and mortality. That perception is implicit in the work of Compton-Burnett. Her central illustration and metonym of creature and condition is the English family, usually the landed gentry and its heritage, dramatised and articulated as a determining force, with characters unusually conscious of their membership of a larger whole.

She presents several generations of Victorian or Edwardian upper-class family living together in the family house, estate or 'place', but also goes beyond the theme of family heritage to consider the brevity and frailty of mortal experience. She follows George Eliot, the first great agnostic novelist, and Thomas Hardy, the first great atheist novelist and poet, who imagined personal identity and experience in a post-Darwinian world without the comfort of metaphysical faith.

In 1938, *Dear Octopus*, a family drama by Dodie Smith, offered an amusing and simple version of organic membership of a family; in 1953, Theodore Sturgeon's utopian novel, *More Than Human*, and in 1969 John Wyndham's *The Midwich Cuckoos* ambitiously invented fantastic organisms with unusual cohesion. Sturgeon's Gestalt creature is composed of individual but interdependent members, while Wyndham's highly evolved 'composite personality' or 'contessarate mind' is a colony without individuals (129; 176). The creature's awareness of its conditions, which is simplified in these fantasies, was internalised by some affective particularities of realist fiction: Hardy's Gabriel Oak in *Far from the Madding Crowd* (1874) and Lawrence's Tom Brangwen in *The Rainbow* (1915) feel they do not belong to themselves but to something larger than self, the phenomenal world in which they live and labour. Their awareness is seen as *ecstasis*, a going-out of self, an experience of freedom and expansion reminiscent of Kant's Sublime, which suspends the sense of comparison.[2] Compton-Burnett's awareness of being part of a larger whole is not fantastic, romantic or sublime. She usually shows it as restrictive, oppressive, uncomfortable, a negation of ecstasy, more like a vastation, in a way resembling Kant's idea but without the raptures of Hardy and Lawrence. Her larger world is historic, social and familial, and her imaginative sense of belonging has not a flicker of aesthetic, sensuous or creative delight in the non-human phenomenal world. Her thinking characters can enjoy life, and unlike Sophocles' choric voice, apparently prefer it to never being born or to dying, but often resent it – bitterly, humorously or drily. Their expansion into relationship, always a family relationship, at times harking back in time, can be a benefit in tolerating and assimilating immorality and crime, and is sometimes appreciated, but it is more often oppressive or frustrating. Samuel Butler, whom she admired, has a relevant note on 'Unity and Separateness':

> The puzzle which puzzles every atom is the same which puzzles ourselves – a conflict of duties – our duty towards ourselves, and our duty as members of a body politic. It is swayed by its sense of being a separate thing – of having a life to itself which nothing can share; it is also swayed by the feeling that in spite of this it is only part of an individuality which is greater than itself and which absorbs it.[3]

Her psychology is original. She endows individual characters with emotional responses to the membership and instrumentality, of which they are aware: pain, anger, resignation, irony, humour, detachment and fulfilment. Hardy and Lawrence imagine characters responding to something larger than their identity; neither author nor character knows the universe glimpsed in sky and stars, its ineffability expressed as an expansive, sublime vision in appropriate language. Compton-Burnett's men and women live in country estates and villages where nature might as well not exist, their experience social, their language not rhapsodic but usually austere.

Compton-Burnett has no time for religious fervour, and Emily Herrick in *Pastors and Masters* jokes about envying the belief in providence and immortality. The novelist proposes no consolations for her average rational and sensual men and women, and though she usually places them in easy material conditions, she is aware of the conditions that circumscribe and shape all mortal lives. At the centre of interest are the rational and sensitive people who share her disbelief; I cannot imagine that her novels are comfortable reading for religious readers. She is not amoral; on the contrary, though her wrong-doers are usually assimilated into the family and forgiven, she casts a cold eye on human cruelty, greed and deceit, though showing them in characters who are either sympathetic or tolerable, confounding readers brought up on the English novelists' preference for simple moral taxonomies. Her rationalists accept the human conditions in their different ways, and such awareness as they possess is felt as personal and familial, not politicised but with political implications. Her sense of the creature's conditioning, like that of the historical consciousness of which it is an aspect, and which emerged in *Vanity Fair*, *Middlemarch* and *Jude the Obscure*, is shown explicitly or implicitly. Its gradual development suggests that she hit on it half-consciously in the course of writing, though, unsurprisingly, it becomes more clearly formulated as she writes on.

In *Dolores* (1911) and *Pastors and Masters* (1925), the power of the family is dramatised but not subsumed in the recognition of larger social organisms like the inherited estate or the great house; here, characters whose lives are shaped by family obligation are not landed gentry and are unconscious of the forces shaping them. Nor are they explicitly shown as historically determined, though the conditioning process is evident once we look for it. *Brothers and Sisters* (1929) places its drama in the manor house of Moreton Edge, and begins with Andrew Stace, a patriarch possessed by house and heritage, who longs to secure and shape their future. The novel is not clearly theme-driven, the sense of social organism not strong or developed. Andrew's descendants are not interested in house and heritage, and the novel ends with his grandchildren eagerly leaving for a London life, their neighbours expecting new inhabitants of the dispossessed estate.

In *Men and Wives* (1931), family relationships are crucial but its plots driven by egocentric characters who do not recognise their membership of a larger organism. *More Women than Men* (1933) is set in a school, and though family life is central, and the novel features one country house and heritage, that part of the action is marginal. The central character, Josephine Napier, is too egocentric to recognise shaping circumstance, though she makes pretty play of her school as a demanding social organism and her submission to its routines and rituals.

The internalised awareness of conditioning circumstance next appears in *A House and Its Head* (1935), where the title's 'House' and the body metaphor 'Head', supported by comment in the novel, signify the arrival of a deeply probed theme. Possible developments were hinted at in previous novels but *A House and Its Head* explicitly presents the family estate as an organism in which individual members are subordinated, for better and worse. The relationship and its consequences are discussed more centrally and thoroughly in *A Family and a Fortune* (1939), less emphatically in *Daughters and Sons* (1937), and centrally in *A Heritage and Its History* (1959), another novel where the idea is introduced by the title. Sporadically or concentratedly, usually not in ways which engross the novel, Compton-Burnett does what I think no other novelist has done, in making characters feel the pressure of social organism and, by implication, of capitalism. In *Vanity Fair*, Thackeray endows his narrator with an awareness of history, and George Eliot internalises historical imagination in Felix Holt, Dorothea and Daniel Deronda.[4] With less conceptual inclination and knowledge, Compton-Burnett psychologised historical consciousness in a greater variety of affective response, showing the debility and energy, positives and negatives, of feeling part of a whole. She articulates the experience as dissolving individual identity and affect; it is as if the body's organs become aware of function, delighting in being arm or leg or nerve doing the brain's will, or resisting instrumentality and subservience.

At times, the subordination is clear to reader but not character. On the first page of *A House and Its Head*, the power of inherited place and property is made explicit, animated but inhuman, large and strange. Critics have, of course, emphasised the dominance of the novel's dramatic and polylogic form but, as we have seen, authorial narration can be important, and the more conspicuous for being rare:

> the room was the usual dining-room of an eighteenth-century country house. The later additions to the room had honourable place, and every opportunity to dominate its character, and used the last in the powerful manner of objects of the Victorian age, seeming in so doing to rank themselves with their possessor. (7)

Ellen and Duncan Edgeworth, husband and wife, tyrant and victim, have been introduced, but the absence of any specification of their dining-room and its furnishings compounds impersonality, as is clear if we think of the expressive objects in Thackeray's rich interiors, or

Mrs Lowder's drawing-room in James's more introverted *Wings of the Dove*. Thackeray's knowing narrator, making an inventory, and James's Merton Densher, daunted by the heavy ornate furniture, are psychologically and morally alert to signs and metonyms of social circumstance. Some characters in *A House and Its Head* possess such awareness but the Edgeworth couple are insensitive to the impersonal, looming power of that house, which the reader reads as both literal and symbolic. Compton-Burnett's sense of historical time across three eras – the eighteenth century, the novel's Victorian past and the twentieth century, identified by a mention of 'the Victorian age' (7) – makes the environment dauntingly enclosed, huge and powerful. The collocation of thing and person in 'House' and 'Head', on title-page and other pages, underlines the theme. The dead metaphor 'Head' is revived in grim enlightenment.

The language and dramatic action dehumanise and animate the material, presented as fantastic, often unpleasantly or uncannily strange – 'uncanny' as in Freud's *'unheimlich'* or 'unhomely', which was brilliantly anticipated by Fontane in *Effi Briest*, where the heroine's lack of a home in a full sense – sexual, domestic and familial – is dramatised in the figure of a foreign ghost which disturbs Effi's homecoming and marital home. Compton-Burnett is no fantasist but she too can show home as unhomely, though not fantastically abnormal.

After we take in title and first scene, the subject disappears from the action for a while, giving way to the strong plot interests of Ellen's death, her husband's re-marriage, and his second wife's infidelity with his nephew and heir. But the deep theme soon re-emerges, to make its impact. The careless, tactless gossip, Dulcia Bode, says, 'Grant with them . . . looking so dear and distinguished . . . as if he were the heir of all he surveyed! Which of course he still is; and may he always be,' provoking Miss Burtonshaw's guarded 'The future will take care of itself', and Grant's more personalised 'That seems to be so . . . It is setting about it' (115). The repeated 'it' brings its own sinister suggestion of powerful impersonality, which returns when Duncan, head of the house, insists that Grant's engagement to his daughter Sibyl will not involve a separate establishment: 'there is room in the house for its life to spread' (190), where the combination of 'its' and 'life' has its strange, scary suggestion of impersonal power. Duncan's complacent welcome of 'life' and 'spread' speaks more for his complicity as head and for the organism's size and power than is comfortable for other characters and the reader. Like other heads of house in the novels, Duncan respects his heir even after he displaces him, but ensures his sustenance and status in the future in a way that suggests the effects of function cannot be easily removed, and is more ominous than reassuring.

The title's emphasis, with its abstract 'House' and metaphorical 'Head', which is also a metonymy for membership, is reinforced in repetition. After his customary bullying of a passive wife, Duncan asks his reasonable daughter, Nance, insubordinately on the woman's side, 'are you the head of the house, or am I?' and she replies, 'Oh, you are, Father; and I want Mother to be' (15). The pathos and horror of the mother's cruelly neglected fatal illness – one of the most appalling episodes in the novels – bears out the feebleness of such attempts to dislodge authority – how can a Head, that indispensable organ, be displaced without the body's death? Events are made more frightening as they shift responsibility from the man's authority to his instrumentality; the Head of a House must dominate.

In *Daughters and Sons* (1937), the emphasis is on membership of family, not house and heritage. That membership, and the subjection of the individual, are dramatised after the death of Sabine Ponsonby, one of the more sympathetic family rulers and not the only tyrant in this novel. When her rule is over, the familiar efficient structure is dissolved, the future of 'the house' unsettled and shapeless:

> The guests made a movement to go . . . They left the room . . . It seemed that they had seen her for some time as at the point of her death. Her son and daughter, rising in their minds as her successors, seemed weak figures, dim and uncertain by Sabine. The house seemed to have a future, dim, flat, smooth, without extremes. (256)

We move from Sabine to her successors, 'the guests', 'They', then 'Her son and daughter'. The novel's emphasis is on family not house but the impersonal house is functional, as the membership changes its functions. The sudden loss of shape after the ending of tyranny is a sideways shift, since her daughter, Hetta, and the more passive son, John, have competed with Sabine for power. The imagery of uncertainty, weakness and dimness is collective, made more unpleasantly strange in vagueness and formlessness, as if the live organism is waiting for individual members to take their place, to restore shape and definition. In context, this impression is stronger because Hetta and John have claimed headship. We move from featureless family organism to the chief claimant: 'Hetta moved from one room to another as mistress of the house. She gave directions, easily, certainly, keeping her eyes from the rest, as if she felt that her self-exposure was lost in what had followed it' (256). The idea of a live, shaping, impersonal presence is powerfully pervasive throughout the book but made explicit only on this occasion, leaving it to the reader to make a more general application in retrospect. Compton-Burnett's novels not only make us re-read sentences or paragraphs but also can make us re-read the novel.

In *A Family and a Fortune* (1939), the idea of conditioning is explicit throughout the novel; we cannot miss it. The social organism here is one often expressed in political and literary discourse as the cash nexus. Hence the clever, compressed title, which can rely on a familiar conflation of good fortune with good investments and income. Compton-Burnett never inhabited or inherited a great house – though some people assumed she had – but she inherited enough property, land and investments to know the connection between financial fortune and other kinds. When she made Dudley Gaveston heir to enough money to buy desirable things, including gratitude and a prospective wife, and also made him see the funny and the terrible side of money but not become obsessed with it, she knew what she was talking about, though she lived in a glass house, and as I have said, misled friends by talk of poverty, applied to the Royal Literary Fund as hard-up author, and surprised everyone by the amount of money she left.

During one long stretch of the action and recurring at the end, the power of money is made explicit, in a study of donation which is chillingly dramatic and particular. Dudley is the uncle who plays second fiddle and money makes him important and interesting. His fortune lets him give, take back and give again. He gives his niece a modest sum for 'her' old men and women, an allowance and pocket money to two nephews, an annuity to his brother's sister-in-law, Matty, and dresses to his sister-in-law and Miss Griffin, Matty's companion-housekeeper; he starts to repair the crumbling old house for his brother and for the heir, and saves the life of Miss Griffin when Matty turns her out in the snow.

Money is abstract and solid, real and imaginary. News of the fortune spreads like wildfire, its size mistaken and exaggerated, as they all ask, 'How much?', highmindedly boasting of not grasping figures, disguising cupidity as generous acceptance, not wanting a share or only a small one, counting, miscounting, calculating, spellbound by numbers. Any fraction of a million seems as good as a million, and sums of money grow huge, meaningless and impersonal, till the sight of the young miser, Clement's, gold coins brings a crude and physical shock. Most novels are about money and this comedy must be one of the best.

A Heritage and Its History (1959) is another novel where the theme of instrumentality and conditioning is elaborately developed and sustained, encompassing money, heritage and class: abstract title emphasises impersonal institution. Several characters show the awareness of something larger than self: Sir Edwin Challoner, head of his house for most of the novel; his brother Hamish, who succeeds him; several women; and the chief character, Simon Challoner, obsessed and driven by his inherited membership of the great house.

At the start, Simon is restless about not being direct heir, blocked by his father, and Hamish, next by being heir and not head; he is finally disinherited by his own illegitimate son, a younger Hamish, conceived in a brief affair with his stepmother. As heir and dispossessed victim, Simon is central to the subject of conditioning: we are now and then distracted by the sensational crises of secret adultery and threatened incest, but the theme is kept in mind by Simon's bitter deprivations and their consequences. Exiled in his wife's house, he threatens his children with homeless poverty, though they repeat resilient jokes about the workhouse.

The theme dominates the novel in the last two chapters, where a new character – Hamish's wife, Marcia – plays a prominent part. She rebels against the dominating house, her resistance making crystal-clear its powers: 'It seems as if nothing had ever been altered here. I suppose nothing has.' Asked temptingly if she wants to change anything, she resists again: 'I could not think of it. Nothing could be different. It would be like something unearthed after ages' (159). She sees the patriarchal threat, internalising a deep feminist insight: 'It will draw me into itself' (159). But she also sees her unfitness to become its inhabitant and instrument, saying 'the house' does not welcome her because she is too old, too plain and not poor enough, recognising the survival of the fittest, reflecting her author's interest in Darwin: 'Someone younger and more dependent would fit the part. And the house would have more welcome for her' (161). She images daunting space and enveloping family – 'All this that surrounds me, and all these relations' – and her final flight with Hamish, the heir, makes house and heritage stronger and stranger (164). Her words are part of an image-pattern of a plant, which reveals the animate but inhuman house in different moods: 'You are bound to this place, that shadows you with a dead past and a threatened future . . . I can never send my roots down here . . .' She is too educated and intelligent, the house 'too large and old' (164–5). Marcia's is a feminist voice but she perceives the subjection of men as well as women, and Hamish shares her fear and comprehension: 'No one could have welcomed me . . . Certainly the house did not' (163).

Simon warmly defends the house – 'It is a grateful house, kind to its inmates, sad to lose them. When I left it, I felt its sympathy, and I still feel it' (162) – but his personification makes the house seem stronger and stranger, less human and more powerful, as its kindness and sympathy solicit the one who will serve it best. Marcia understands: 'I knew it was human. I must simply resist its hold. I cannot be bound and burdened. I must be free and travel light. I shall live in it, an alien' (162). But she goes, taking Hamish from his heritage to die without offspring, and leaving Simon to inherit, the house desiring him as he desired it. Finally, he enters into full possession, in love with Marcia, who returns his feeling; they are opposites, magnetised like elective affinities.

Feminist critique returns in a conversation between two sisters, Rhoda and Simon's wife, Fanny, re-emphasising the impersonal power:

'So you are to live in the house, and I am to leave it,' said Rhoda. 'Which of us is fortunate?'

'Neither of us . . . We have known the place and served it. We have seen it regarded as something it could not be. As a force in the background, with human lives helpless in the fore. And that is not what it is. It may be so in some minds . . . not in yours or mine . . .' (170)

The place is further defamiliarised as it is imaged as a strange space with dark, haunted corners feared by the young children, and Simon voices the irony – 'Emma and Claud find their nursery too much for them. When I feel they are at last in their home', his son Ralph adding, 'The question of home is always ominous for us' (175). Still questioning the patriarchal power she cannot escape, Fanny says it 'is strange that a house should absorb a human being' and, of course, Simon disagrees – 'Did something tell me that my place was here, that my service to it made it mine?' – and 'something' is another impersonalising touch (179). Soon after, his word 'service' is echoed, and the mystique of the masterful House qualified in class terms by the butler Deakin, who knows all about service: 'there was dependence on the large house' (180). The servant class opposes what it has to serve and sometimes accepts unthinkingly, but this manservant's words underline and refine Simon's metaphor.

As place and master–servant join their unequal forces, the place gathers strength. This is emphasised in the family gathering after Hamish, the dead heir, is buried in the family vault, and Simon's family comes home, 'feeling they had reached a settled stage in their lives' (184). There is a ritualised conclusion when Claud and Emma come in, bearing a garland to celebrate their acceptance of a house no longer haunted: 'we like this house, now we are used to it.' Asked how they have achieved this, they answer, 'Just by belonging to the family . . . We rise and fall together' (186). Hamish has gone but Simon's legitimate descendants accept their part in the whole, and they may remind us of Oak's and Brangwen's expansive joy in something larger than themselves. In this ceremony, the heir and his progeny submit to historical circumstance, part perfectly fitting whole, the conditioned creature in the right place. It is a renewal for the house, and a historically realistic conclusion. It was imagined by an artist who was superficially conservative, though deeply, if not always consciously, aware of social organism. Never a member of a great house, she had experienced membership of a family, and transferred the experience to different circumstances. No doubt she had experienced accepting and resisting the family, and observed her siblings and half-sisters doing so too.

The radical emphasis on subordination to history, in the form of a future as well as a past, returns in *The Last and the First* (1971), where there is once again the sense of being a part of something larger than the personal self. Sir Robert Heriot, head of a house, says, 'This house is a living thing to me. It seems to carry the other lives, whose legacy is in my own . . . I feel I leave it something of myself'. He knows this is no ordinary idea: 'It may be false and foolish and untrue. It is my own truth' (106). His second wife, Eliza, is wiser than she knows – 'The future must have time to take its shape. It can't form in a moment' – and her rebellious step-daughter, Hermia, answers without pain or pleasure, 'It is taking it. I hardly have to think of it' (115). Both women formulate the future as an impersonal presence, which shapes and changes their lives. The story ends with the restoration of the household, which is threatened by financial loss and saved by Hermia's inheritance from a man who proposes to her, is rejected and dies. She is willing to play a benign and vital part, making terms with her tyrant in no simple, easy spirit of reconciliation but to serve family and future. Political implications are more overt in *A Family and a Fortune* and *A Heritage and Its History* but the recognition of the subordination of creature to circumstance here encourages a political application.

Direct statements of the theme are reinforced by indirections of language and symbol. In *A Heritage and Its History*, Simon feels the creeper outside the window as an encroaching presence. In *A Father and His Fate*, Miles is asked why he did not destroy an incriminating envelope which reveals his intended bigamy, and says he felt the object as a daunting animated presence; the excuse conveys his grandiose desire to shift responsibility but reinforces the sense of contingency. There is recurring meta-drama: characters feel that they are performing, part of a scene or characters in a story, and they 'really' act, in mimes, charades and games which intensify the sense of creatures formed by circumstance. Important too is the choric conversation in which family members collaborate, often without the speakers' names, in collective speech appropriate for a body of related members, mere parts of a whole.

Consciously, unconsciously and originally, the novelist uses her art to embody and particularise a radical concept.

Notes

1. Henry James, *The Critical Muse: Selected Literary Criticism*, 423.
2. Immanuel Kant, *Critique of Judgment*, §25–7.
3. Samuel Butler, *Notebooks*, 143.
4. See Barbara Hardy, '*Middlemarch*: Public and Private Worlds', in *Particularities: Readings in George Eliot*.

Chapter 6

Meals and Hospitalities

Eve and Adam ate the apple, Jacob and Esau argued over a mess of pottage, Jesus changed water to wine and held the Last Supper, the Macbeths entertained Duncan before murdering him, Thackeray criticises conspicuous consumption in 'comic' feasts that turn dreary or violent,[1] Pip, the blacksmith's apprentice, is a perfect host, Magwitch, the convict, a grateful guest, and Pip's sister a harsh housekeeper.[2] Compton-Burnett has her own peculiar version of storms in tea-cups and mad-hatters' tea-parties where domestic routines signify values, emotions and relationships. At first sight, her English, upper-middle-class meals seem circumstantially realistic, but routines become rituals, surfaces stage microdrama, china and cutlery provide props and symbols. Domestic life becomes altogether more expressive as it is displayed for our inspection – of course, not always systematically or consciously. Compton-Burnett has the re-creative power to make ordinary things look extraordinary, which Coleridge compared to the effect of moonlight on familiar landscape[3] and the Russian formalist, Viktor Shklovsky, called 'ostranenie' (estrangement or 'enstrangement').[4] The dailiness of life is enlarged or changed, as if seen through a microscope or in slow motion, serving history, politics and art.

The story often starts with breakfast, the beginning of the novel nicely coinciding with the beginning of the day. The details are familiar: greetings, unpunctuality, bad temper, over-sleeping, not sleeping, tea, coffee, toast, rolls, fish and meat. In *Pastors and Masters*,[5] there is a comic breakfast in the basement dining-room of the fifth-rate private school, with routines of 'Good Morning', morning exchanges between the never-sincere Mr Merry and his tea-pouring wife, and complaints from faddy boys:

'Will you have tea or coffee, dear?' said Mrs Merry.

'Oh, either, either; anything will do for me.'

'I always arrange for you to have your choice, dear.'

'Yes, Mother; yes. You take good care of me.' . . .

. . . 'Mrs Merry,' Miss Basden said, in a rather high monotone, 'the boys are saying that the marmalade is watery. I am telling them that no water is used in marmalade, that marmalade does not contain water; so I do not see how it can be.' (7)

Next on the scene is unpunctual Mr Burgess, the only qualified teacher,[6] whose breakfast has been kept warm by Fanny, the maid, with more gratitude from Merry: 'Thank you, Fanny, very much,' where every comma is eloquent.[7] He is followed by Nicholas Herrick, the inactive Head and owner of the fifth-rate private school, speeding through prayers. Burgess enjoys the bacon and asks a boy to get his newspaper: 'It matters very little to me what time I breakfast' (7). Another breakfast is staged at the dismal and unpunctual table of the tyrannical Reverend Henry Bentley, whose sons attend Herrick's school, and later on we see him trying to get some sense out of Merry at a prize day, where boys serve tea, teachers tell lies to parents, and Mrs Merry graces 'a table furnished by a consistence of fate with cups and an urn' (51).

Ending the novel and the day is a comic dinner-party where the everyday use of school-rooms is disguised, and the only consumable specified is coffee supplied by Mrs Merry, whose disappearance to make it is mistaken for exhausted escape. She is the 'Mother', whose Christian name (Emily) we only learn at this late stage, the archetypal desperate housekeeper: 'I should like there to be no such thing as food, myself' (90). The not very clever teacher Miss Basden addresses the company: 'I never can remember to eat, myself . . . If I can remember, I always do, because I think one can do so much more, if one eats' (91).

Brothers and Sisters begins with Andrew Stace, who is 'over eighty':

'Fetch another glass, and don't fill it over the brim,' he said to his servant, frowning with no less bitterness against old age, that he had taken every care to attain it . . .

The second glass met the misfortune of the first, and Andrew set it hard on the table, as if to punish fate by making it overreach.

'Ah, I am a wretched old creature, spilling and shaking as if I were just out of my cradle or my grave.' (6)

The two overfilled wineglasses image irascible old age, to start a story of ruling passions and dark secrets. Thirty years later, in the next chapter, Andrew's daughter Sophia heads the table on her elder son's twenty-fifth birthday, celebrated by a good breakfast and guests for tea and dinner, none of which he enjoys. Tea is for unwanted cousins and dinner for desirable friends but the poor relations will hang round. In the after-dinner retrospect, a ritual in the novels, Dinah, the daughter of the house, says if prayers were answered, cousin Peter Bateman's son, Latimer, would have been struck by lightning as he went in to dinner unsuitably dressed and on his father's arm. Bad hostess is mismatched with bad guest, like rogue with gull in Ben Jonson, as Peter returns Sophia's grudging hospitality with rude manners, spilling tea, outstaying his welcome, and grunting a cursory 'Goodbye, all' (51).

The main plot turns on threatened incest, actual incest, a burnt will and a mislaid letter; the affective action concerns demanding mother and harassed children; the sub-plot featuring the tactless, gossiping Peter and his pathetic family is travesty and background. Comic meals give way to tragic ones. After Christian Stace's funeral, dinner is organised by the housekeeper–companion, Patty, who 'watched the setting of the table' and led the widow to her seat:

> 'No, I won't have anything to eat,' said Sophia . . . 'I will just try to drink a glass of wine.'
>   The five sat silent, the young people at the end of their strength. Patty made a few attempts at talk, but when Sophia spoke, it was not to respond.
>   'I don't know whether you all like sitting there, having your dinner, with your mother eating nothing? On this day of all days!' (135)

Patty reminds her she chose not to eat but hurries 'to her side with food', Sophia says she needs a little pressing, 'sitting here, as I am, with my life emptied', the children cannot respond, Patty goes on offering food, Sophia tries blackmail – 'that would be the only thing that would persuade me, somebody's caring' – and the children do their best except for Robin, who says his mother is not a child and 'made a very fair luncheon'. This appeases Sophia because it shows 'observation of her' (136).

Meals punctuate and promote the action in main plot and gossips' chorus. Their neighbour, Julian Wake, gives a tea-party to satisfy his insatiable curiosity – 'we can't put gossip off' (91). His party features sensational gossip, columbines he grew, cut and arranged, farewell flowers for Tilly, an awkward exit from Peter, a host's verdict – 'a dreadful tea-party . . . a most humiliating unsuccess', and a final request to his sister not to 'put the saucers together on the top of the spoons' as he cheers himself with a 'real tidy-up' (100). Two chapters later, Julian asks another neighbour to host another tea-party: 'I can't always give these dubious parties' (144).

In *More Women than Men*, social occasions include several ruined by another self-indulgent widow, Josephine Napier, better and worse than Sophia and Harriet for being insincere. The novel and new term start with Josephine sending her staff one by one to be strengthened by tea in the senior common room, where recurring mini-dramas make more play with guest–host relations. Deferential teachers entertain deferential Head, who does not make things easier by being unable to see a joke or manage a light touch:

> 'This room is not in my province: it is good of you to make me welcome in it. And I don't know why I should have the easiest chair, unless it is because I am the guest. I should certainly give it to any of you in my rooms. Well, they did not play me false in the matter of the springs . . . Miss Munday, I believe I am turning you out of it?' . . .
>
> 'Are we going to send for another cup?' said Josephine to Miss Munday, somehow attaining a decision, but hesitating to take upon herself the office of hostess . . .
>
> 'Will you bring another cup and saucer, please?' said Miss Munday to the maid.
>
> 'Thank you,' said Josephine to Miss Munday.
>
> 'We have hot scones on the day when our head comes to tea,' said Miss Luke.
>
> 'You always have hot things brought to you, I hope?' . . .
>
> . . . 'I meant, we did not always have this kind,' said Miss Luke.
>
> 'I hope you send for any kind you prefer,' said Josephine . . . (79–80)

Josephine asks if she is to 'come first' and Mrs Chattaway says, '"Well, I should think so" . . . running forward with the sugar and tongs, and for the last steps without the tongs.' The little farce goes on and on: Josephine covers the clumsiness by 'taking some sugar with her fingers, as if unconscious of another method'; Mrs Chattaway runs 'back for the tongs, and forward again to Josephine, as if the latter also might remedy her omission'; the guest says, 'Yes, I will have a little more sugar. Thank you'; and there is a joke from Miss Munday – 'It is a pity we only have four meals a day,' which is lost on Mrs Chattaway – 'I should be sorry to have any more . . . I can hardly manage those there are.' More desperate quips are made and lost: '"It would be unsocial," said Mrs Chattaway,' to a suggestion that meals could be missed, and '"It would indeed", said Josephine, "And what is more, it would be very bad for you"' (80–1). This storm in the tea-cups is comedy and synecdoche: the polite guest who uses her beringed fingers instead of sugar-tongs is capable of lies, husband-stealing and killing. Compton-Burnett is often compared with Oscar Wilde, and this scene recalls the cucumber sandwiches, bread and butter, cake and sugar lumps in *The Importance of Being Earnest*.

In *A House and Its Head*, the psycho-drama is ominous when the beautiful Alison Edgeworth, second wife of the bullying Duncan, meets his family. The tea ceremony begins with Duncan's sharp tone, used 'to cover his consciousness' – 'Nance, are we not to have tea?' – and when Nance offers her 'place', Alison demurs – 'You ought to pour it out . . . I will put off all duties while excuse offers', then sinks on to a sofa, 'looking from face to face' (120). Her nonchalance signals a contrast with her predecessor, who began the novel by coming to breakfast cowed and deferential, and was forced to attend meals as she was dying. Alison shows her wanton ways with her ageing husband: 'She took the cup in one hand, and reaching for Duncan's hand with the other, swung it caressingly, while Duncan's family kept their eyes from his face.' She rises to greet Cassie, the housekeeper, 'stooping over Duncan, with her hands on his shoulders', and charmingly accepts more: 'Oh yes, please; cups and cups.' As Grant, the heir, to be one of her lovers, brings the tea, she looks at him: 'Of course you are all distinguished looking' (120–1).[8] Every word, move and look signifies character and spins plot, all among the tea-cups.

Emily Herrick in *Pastors and Masters* says, 'It must be terrible to do good' (40), and self-indulgent do-gooders star in the chorus of *A House and Its Head*. Beatrice laughingly expects many cups of tea when she brings the neighbours her personal Christmas message but her friend Dulcia does better, making the rounds to announce the birth of the Edgeworth baby, getting, as she hopes, 'a good deal of refreshment in the course of my peregrinations' (143). Her first call is unnecessary because it brings the news to the doctor who delivered the baby, but he is hospitable:

'You will share our breakfast, Miss Dulcia?' . . .
    'Well, I believe I will, Doctor,' said Dulcia, glancing about the table. 'I left home after a very light meal, to be betimes with my news, and now I find it is not news, I am conscious of an emptiness.' (144)

'Settling her sleeves, and addressing herself to the board', she says the next neighbour can wait 'better than my morning appetite, whetted by a walk and a sense of having taken a fall', and falls to: 'By Jove, these mushrooms are what they ought to be!' (144–5). As she devours her food with the gusto of Dickens's Chadband in *Bleak House*, we know what she does not know, that the father of Alison's newborn baby is not her husband. The reader triumphs over the village gossip.

In *Daughters and Sons*, the family is introduced at breakfast, presided over in breath-taking style by Sabine, who greets the day and her grandchild, Muriel, with 'Well, gapy-face' (5). She summons her older grandchildren with a rap on the window, ordering one to bring her glasses and footstool, and another to take medicine for a dull manner and complexion. She tells off another for not reading prayers, another for carving pheasant breast for himself, and the governess for oversleeping:

> The family waited while Miss Bunyan ate, having less to look at than was natural in the circumstances, as she made hardly perceptible motions of her mouth, as though seeing mastication as one of those things which are inevitable but better passed over. (11)

Her biscuits at night make Muriel giggle, and begin a running joke about the governess's appetite. Clare observes, 'It is odd how we always get round to meals' but Sabine replies, 'It is not at all odd. Meals must always be a great part of life, the first object of a woman's thought, of servants' work, of a man's income' (22). Compton-Burnett's meals are part of her social surface, their disruptions of ceremony comic and serious registers of class and family tensions.

In the innumerable meals of this novel, food is often specified: bacon, pheasant and marmalade for breakfast, cold lamb for one luncheon, chicken for another, milk-break or 'mid-morning luncheon' for governess and pupil, and two baked eggs for Miss Bunyan's tea when she is excluded from a family dinner: 'I have to compress two meals into one . . . It sounds quite a feat of skill' (34). The governess is the vicar's niece and her subservience one of status rather than class, but the hierarchy is still political. Muriel laughs at the defensive joke but the hapless eater goes on 'in an educational tone': 'We must not get into the way of feeling self-conscious over having reasonable appetites. That is a piece of foolishness which we have grown out of, which only exists in the lower classes now' (34–5). The oppression ends in her resignation, after which she adopts 'a note of equality', is ordered to resume her former style, then with Sabine's 'hands actually on the chicken', declares: 'I will not have any more. I will eat and drink no more in this house' (55). It is as dramatic and political as Oliver Twist's demand for more gruel, and like it in showing the table as battlefield. The next governess, Edith Hallam, said by the perceptive tutor, Alfred, to have 'a little touch of the guest' about her (122), expects to be well fed without bringing her own biscuits and is happy to share some meals alone with her pupil. Her demeanour and her reception reflect on the humiliations and triumph of her predecessor, extending the drama and history of domestic oppressions.

Sabine's grandchildren, Chilton and Victor, are welcomed by hospitable neighbours after their grandmother tells them to wait out of sight outside because they are 'too many to come to tea' (77) and a single detail shows Chilton resisting more effectively than Miss Bunyan, just 'stirring his cup' (78). At supper after the village play, Miss Bunyan, no longer a governess, is a self-possessed hostess, never referring to her past lowly position at Sabine's table. When the tutor drops a hot and handleless coffee-pot, provoking heavy joking by the vicar, his author may possibly have been thinking of Henry James, to whom she was often compared and whom she admired, with reservations.[9]

Meals seldom pass without incident, but drama is not always at such a high pitch. It resumes at a dinner-party, where the host, John Ponsonby, apologises for disregarding 'the laws of civility' by talking about himself (134); he has received a cheque from an anonymous admirer of his novels – actually his daughter, France, whom he has jealously tried to stop writing. Speculation animates the table-talk but the party ends with another incivility when Sabine, the hostess, memorably asks, 'Are they never going?' (149) and the fascinated guests rise to the occasion, 'We have so enjoyed the evening . . . We are so very sorry we came' (151). The final violation of ceremony is another dinner-party, which begins with a guest observing 'it is such a good idea to give a dinner, when you have been supposed to be dead' (237), Sabine saying her family look as if they are at a funeral (240), and repeating her insult 'gapy face' to a guest (251). Dinner continues with malice and muddle over seating. France asks, 'Why did we have this dinner?' (248) but sees their guests are more entertained than embarrassed. Then, as the host says, 'This cannot go on,' it does: his sister, Hetta, gets to her feet and makes a 'harsh' speech 'torn from some depth within her below the level of speech' (252). She lets the skeletons out: Sabine persuaded her son to marry the new governess for her supposed earnings as a novelist and France is the prize-winning benefactor. And the party is not over. The tutor moves to make kind conversation to Sabine, and she does not reply because she is dead.

In *A Family and a Fortune*, the novel begins with a less determined autocrat presiding at breakfast:

> 'Justine, I have told you that I do not like the coffee touched until I come down. How can I remember who has had it, and manage about the second cups, if it is taken out of my hands? I don't know how many times I have asked you to leave it alone.'
>
> 'A good many, Mother dear, but you tend to be rather a laggard. When the poor boys sit in thirsty patience it quite goes to my heart.' (7)

There is expressive summary:

> Justine and Mark conversed with goodwill and ate with an ordinary appetite; Clement did not converse and showed an excellent one; Blanche watched her children's plates and made as good a meal as she could without giving her attention to it, and Aubrey sat and swung his feet and did not speak or eat.

Blanche protests and Aubrey says with a smile, 'If I have some toast, perhaps I shall grow tall enough to go to school'; sour Clement complains that the 'omelette is surely a breach with tradition', to be told by his mother, 'without looking at it', that 'it is very good and very wholesome' (9). They eat and drink in character:

> 'Why do you eat it, if you don't like it?' said Mark, with no sting in his tone.
>
> 'I am hungry: I must eat something.'
>
> 'There is ham,' said Justine.
>
> 'Clement will eat the flesh of the pig,' said Aubrey.
>
> 'It is certainly odd that civilised people should have it on their tables,' said his brother.
>
> 'Do uncivilised people have things on tables?'
>
> 'Now, little boy, don't try to be clever,' said Justine, in automatic reproof, beginning to cut the ham. (10)

Blanche's sister, Matty, is critical, jealous and cruel to her companion, Miss Griffin (though once they enjoy a hot bedtime drink in a kind of amity), but after she moves to the lodge in her sister's grounds, there is a celebratory dinner-party. Matty is a bad guest but starts off in a good mood and gracious style:

> 'What a really beautiful room, dear!' said Matty with appreciation brought to birth by the lights and wine and the presence of Dudley and Edgar. 'It is like a little glimpse of home, or if I may not say that, it is like itself and satisfying indeed to my fastidious eye. And my own little room seems to gain, not lose by comparison. This one seems to show how beauty is everywhere itself. I quite feel that I have taken a lesson from it.' (74)

She is excited by the headiness and glamour. Lights and wine and male company make her nostalgic for lost luxury, and stir susceptibilities; a nice detail reverses seniority in 'Dudley and Edgar' to show her preference for the richer and the unmarried man. But there is no such thing as a perfect party: as the guest of honour notices, the butler has no help and Blanche says they need to cut back on staff, Matty smiles derisively, Justine goes on the defensive, others join in, and the outsiders relish their *Schadenfreude*. Like Thackeray, Compton-Burnett knows parties can easily turn nasty, but Matty enjoys the limelight even more than quarrelling and says she is expecting a house-guest. The guest arrives, the evening passes, and the company leaves the family to miscellaneous retrospect: 'I do hope Matty enjoyed the evening' . . . 'I have enjoyed every minute of the evening, but there is nothing more exhausting than a thorough-going family function' . . . 'You need not work so hard at it' . . . 'Yes, anyhow I have done my best. I could spare myself a good deal if I had some support' . . . 'You ought to come out of yourself a little and try to support the talk' . . . 'Is it worthy of any effort?' . . . 'I was so proud of them all . . . I do see that Matty has much less than I have. I ought to remember it.' . . . 'Don't sit up too long' (94–6).

Blanche leaves Edgar and Dudley to smoke: 'We must be a little later than Blanche means . . . I want to talk about how Matty behaved. Better than usual, but so badly' (96). They get on to Matty's guest, Miss Sloane, then Clement, and last Dudley: 'To tell you the truth, I feel so young myself that I hardly feel I am any older than he is'. Dudley discloses his inheritance: 'And now I have made one confession, the ice is broken and I should be able to make another' (97). This is self-generative narration, stories leading to stories and stories within stories.

In *Elders and Betters*, the first meal is in the warm kitchen, hot muffins on moving day, especially enjoyed by Bernard, who needs 'full and frequent meals to avoid fatigue' (21). There is a scrap supper of cold meat, and when Bernard is told the vegetables will be hot, he quips that he has never heard of cold ones. Next day, Cook warms muffins for upstairs tea, and is praised by Ethel and Jenney to the vexation of Anna: 'Is nothing farther removed from Cook than her natural duties?' (28). Every meal tells us something about everyone, but most conspicuous is a family luncheon where Tullia thinks they are thirteen at table, and everyone stands, to reveal superstition and self-interest, till it turns out that they are fourteen. In spite of this, there may be a sinister twist when Jessica, who sits down first, dies soon afterwards, as superstition foretells. This is the least solidly specified long meal in all the novels, with no detail of food, or of the service provided by servants who are never named or mentioned, and a very strange meal indeed.

Manservant and Maidservant turns on frugal housekeeping so most of its meals are sorry affairs. Unlike *Elders and Betters*, it is a novel where meals form an insistent pattern. The breakfast which begins the novel is held up because a jackdaw is stuck in the chimney and the fire is smoking, then breakfast begins with Mortimer Lamb's joke about smoked ham, and his comment on having no choice between tea and coffee, the first hint of his cousin, Horace's, parsimony. The women's breakfast is put to warm, and we hear that Charlotte, mistress of the house whose money is managed by her husband, prefers to leave the frugal housekeeping to her sister-in-law. There is an acrimonious dinner with prolonged discussion of an extra cutlet, followed by the houseboy, Simon's, theft of pudding for himself and unspecified foodstuff intended as a present for friends. (Simon was born in a workhouse and is compared to Oliver Twist.) At Christmas there is no detail of food, except a comment that it is better than usual; there are guests, and Horace is said to use his rare hospitability as a cover for his meanness. The children's deprivation is a running motif. One bag of sweets from Avery's stocking is first shared and then swapped. Once at the nursery table, there is buttered toast, a rare treat: '"You have used a pound of butter," said Nurse; "I do not know what the master would say"' (47). Jasper dares to ask his father for some 'stale cake', pronounced as one word 'as staleness was the condition of their having it' (47); Nurse discovers that Jasper has pocketed a slice because 'One side of the cake is newly cut, and it is only used for guests'; and the scene ends when Horace has 'an impulse to approach a point of danger', asks if Nurse had any cake, and she says, 'I did not want any, sir. I had some bread and butter and a cup of tea. That is my meal ... And there was only enough for the children' (49). Her role in the tea-drama anticipates a later crisis when she heroically reassures and defends the children as the one who knows them best.

Details of frugal living are confined to the dining-room and school-room, but there is drama at the kitchen table where a village shopkeeper, Miss Buchanan, who cannot read and write, is now and then entertained to tea, at the suggestion of kind Mortimer, who guesses her secret. There is ceremony and a disturbance of ceremony, more domestic detail made deep and strange. The hospitality in the sub-plot involves significant specification: the pouring of tea, choice of jam from labelled pots, and a wine-list are domestic details that are fraught for the guest and the observant, kind cook, the impish butler tempted to expose the illiteracy, and the shrewd houseboy from the workhouse who eventually does so. There is a classical recognition scene, followed by a happy ending in which the round, red kitchen-maid from the orphanage agrees to become Miss Buchanan's teacher.

Horace's cruel meanness is dramatised in these meals, but near the end of the novel a cup of tea shows his change, moral and physical. He has been mean about fires, removing coal that burns too bright, but at this tea-time he comes 'to the fire, his face lighting at the sight':

> Bullivant exchanged a glance with Mortimer and went to fetch the tea.
>
> 'This cold seems to have no end,' said Horace.
>
> 'We were on the verge of succumbing to it . . . Bring the tray to the fire, Bullivant; it does not waste the heat to feel it.' . . .
>
> . . . 'Something hot to drink makes people warm,' said Horace, in an unfamiliar tone, speaking with a shiver and looking for a place to set his cup, as though he feared to spill it. Bullivant took it from his hand, as if he had been in readiness to do so. (277)

A little later, he 'put out his hand to his cup, and withdrew it, rested his eyes on the trembling hand, as if it were a thing apart from himself' (278).

This is the second occasion when we see Horace sensuously responsive; there is an earlier episode when he cracks and eats walnuts from their garden, and Charlotte imagines how the children would enjoy them. Like the pudding, the cutlet, the toast and the cake, the warm tea in the full cup is an ordinary thing which speaks volumes, and the unsteady hand on the cup registers a change which is outside and inside, in the man, the weather and the language: 'The cold held, bound the earth, could not break. Fires through the house were piled and deep. Fear of cold had become a different thing; suffering from cold belonged to a past that was distant' (278). The word 'unfamiliar' is used of the sick man's tone but everything about the man and this tea-time by the fireside is made unfamiliar, in a rare passage where Compton-Burnett's prose rises to poetry. We may remember the end of 'The Dead' in *The Dubliners*; though Joyce builds a long, intense dynamic, imaging music, love, graveyard and falling snow, Compton-Burnett uses a small, everyday object, the cup of tea, made strange for the sick man and for us.

On the first page of *Two Worlds and Their Ways*, the contented wife and mother, Maria Shelley, says, 'Meals are such a waste of time' and her husband's reply is good-tempered:

> 'Any congenial way of spending it tends to be called that.'
>   'I wish we could do without them, or without so many.'
> 'The wish is often fulfilled in your case.'
>   'I only eat to keep up my energy.'
> 'You attain your object.' (5)

Everything they do and say at this first breakfast shows their difference and their amity, his easy care and her casual housekeeping:

> Maria's hand encountered the coffee-pot and closed on it. Her husband pushed a cup beneath it and pursued the uncertain stream, and as he withdrew it, tilted the spout to a safe angle. She gave him a glance at the suggested waste of energy, and filled her own cup before she put the pot down.
>   'Thank you, my pretty,' he said, and stirred his cup. (5)

They are joined by the governess–companion and Maria offers hot rolls with friendly tactlessness – 'they ought to be finished today – that is why my husband and I are struggling with them', to be politely answered that they make a nice change from toast. Clemence and Sefton join their parents because the school-room wall is being repaired. They arrive late because they thought 'the breakfast might come up. It is sometimes late', and Maria asks, 'Would you like to go somewhere where you would learn to rely more on yourselves?' Clemence notices letters on the table from their father's relatives, school-teachers who have 'written again' about sending the children to their boarding-schools. Aldom, a servant with eyes as blue as his master's, winks at the children, gossips officiously about the workmen, is told off, takes a dish away and comes back, aware that the children have been rebuked for exchanging glances with him; they are told to 'get on with . . . breakfast' (17). But it is all quite relaxed. Maria presides at tea-time, careful enough to rebuke

Aldom for mismanaging urn and heat, and grumbling good-humouredly about all the cups of tea she has to pour out. The children will move into the different world of school, but we are given a sufficient look at this one in its casual, adaptable, contented, daily routine, sustenance and community.

Not much is made of domestic discomfort at school. There is a tea-time scene, with clever school-girl talk about the tea-bell 'that almost inebriates', and a teacher's appetite. The girls quote, 'There was an old woman and what do you think?', and joke about Clemence being homesick and choking on 'every mouthful' of victuals and drink (91–3). The end-of-term party is mentioned but not shown, and clothes are more important than meals. In Sefton's school, we return to the unap-petising meals of *Pastors and Masters*, and the importance of children's tastes; there is the recurring antipathy to fat, as a new boy told to eat the butter on the top of potted meat is sickened by the smell of it on his handkerchief. The episodes are brief reminders of ease and plenty, and when the children leave school, after disgrace and misery, we return to home comforts.

When the Shelleys invite the children's school-friends to spend the day, lunch is arranged without formality or fuss, Sefton at the top of the table, the girls together at one side, and Sir Roderick, the good host, carrying the 'implements' (262) round the table and chatting hospitably to boys and girls (especially the girls), food unspecified: 'And, of course, they liked the things to eat' (303). The benign retrospect begins with Sir Roderick's '"And how did the host and hostess enjoy it?" . . . "Very much . . . and so did they all"' (303). It is arranged by loving parents for peace and reconciliation, and the sense of hospitable ease spreads to an unusually happy ending. Clemence and Sefton have returned to their old world, though with a loss of innocence. Nobody is perfect: parents are guilty of pride, theft and lust, children lie and cheat, Father has an eye for the girls, the girls and boys do not socialise at the party, the parents do not know about the children's pranks with the servants. But there is love, comfort, security and fun at home, keeping the promise of the first breakfast.

Meals in *Darkness and Day* begin on a dull morning when Sir Ransom Chace and his unmarried daughters welcome their old friend, Grant Lovat, who drops in for a casual visit. Mildred Hallam, 'house-keeper, companion and attendant-friend' (15), invites him to luncheon, which she will 'adapt', Emma Chace wonders what the cook would say, Mildred ripostes that she will 'think out the meal, and order it, and eventually dispense it', so 'do all but prepare it' (23). After lunch, Gaunt meets the maid, Jennet, and congratulates her on 'an excellent pie', which she insists she has only 'carried . . . and handed', and he replies, 'Well, you handed it very well . . . I always enjoy coming to luncheon here' (50). The meal has been presented only in conversation, where Mildred plays a central part. Class distinction is a delicately touched subject when she is patronised for a clever remark about potatoes and peaches, betrays insecurity by excessive confidence, and tells her story of youthful problems and apparent recovery, with a mixture of candour and self-deception. On a later occasion, when the whole Lovat family come to tea and she is asked not to join them, she shrugs off the snub but, in the event, dodges in and out to organise the seating, bring fresh tea, and break a Dresden tea-cup by casually swinging it while she boasts of careful handling. Like the broken coffee-pot at the village show in *Daughters and Sons*, the smashed cup has ancestors in Silas Marner's broken pot and Maggie Verver's golden bowl. The invitation to Grant and the broken cup are important for Mildred's portrait as an adopted illegitimate child, awkward, self-congratulatory and rootless but finding a kind of resolution. She is one of many Compton-Burnett characters who turns out to be more complex than we expect, what E. M. Forster, in *Aspects of the Novel*, called a flat character capable of surprising us, like Bumble shedding a tear for Oliver Twist and indolent Lady Bertram roused by her son's illness in *Mansfield Park*. The central action in which Mildred is involved is with her charming and clever pupils, Rose and Viola, the terrors who turn out to be her half-sisters, but the meals she organises and joins, one way or another, as neither host nor guest, are dramas which unfold her weakness and strength, and bring out the recurring class theme.

The children in *Manservant and Maidservant* love cake and buttered toast, and so do Rose and Viola, devils in the school-room, angels in the kitchen. In spite of what the nurse calls 'the leanness of the land' (*Darkness and Day* 91) – we see why Gaunt enjoyed that pie – the children like the plain cake and scones, and the meals in this novel are good. The very best meal in it, and in all the novels, consists of sixteen pieces of bread toasted on toasting-forks by an open kitchen fire, suggested, made and distributed by the children with care and pleasure. They have looked forward to tea in the kitchen; their hostess – the cook, Mrs Spruce – loves them (for more reasons than first meet the eye), and when she presses more food on them, Rose says she would like to make a slice of toast, and the toast-party begins. The toast-making is a transformation but not a distortion of what is unromantic and ordinary. When the guests, who have been hosts, leave, they are prompted by their nurse to say thank you and give a return invitation. The occasion is an impromptu after-tea treat, made into a ceremony, ritualised by the formal pattern of beginning, middle and end, with perfect manners on everyone's part – and most of the participants show bad manners at other times. It is a short, simple meal which becomes an orderly feast, where for a few moments everyone is happy, everyone considered equally, everyone appreciative, an occasion of warmth, enjoyment and classless interchange for cooks, hosts and guests, relived with pleasure when the girls tell their mother about it in the ritual retrospect. It is too everyday to be called a sacrament, both ordinary and extraordinary, a brief love-feast. But it is not romanticised: as the children make toast, the grown-ups discuss the rumour of their parents' incest, though the good and bad gossip – a distinction made when the children's nurse says the incest story is not gossip to her – has led to the discovery that the rumour is unfounded.

At the beginning of *The Present and the Past*, five brothers, sisters, half-brothers and half-sisters are given cake, which three-year-old Toby generously feeds to a dying hen being pecked by its fellows, Toby eating the bits that fall on the ground, and his brother Gavin uttering his melancholy refrain, 'Oh, dear, oh, dear!', the novel's first words (5). Nursery meals are hilarious, with a plate smashed by Toby and fragments broken in smaller bits by his brothers and sisters. In the dining-room, a tragi-comic displacement is played out at the luncheon table, where Cassius Clare melodramatises the imminent return of his first wife to the house where he lives discontentedly with his second. As one of his children perceives, Cassius is unhappy so wants everyone else to be unhappy, and he laments 'Another meal! . . . The same faces, the same voices, the same things said. I daresay the same food.' When his father jokes about him always bringing his own voice and face to the table, he goes further: '"I wonder if we could dispense with meals . . ." said Cassius, using a sincere tone . . . "We might dispense with luncheon. The children have it upstairs, and older people do not need so much to eat"' (24). His father and wife, Flavia, play along, his father suggesting a tray in his room, his wife admitting 'she might say she wanted to eat in the middle of the day' (24). The serious joking transforms the meal, Cassius breathing 'rather deeply' as he carves, offering his wife her portion ungraciously – 'Will you have any of this?' and 'A good deal, isn't it?' – to which she replies that it is 'an average amount'. After several changes of subject, Cassius succumbs, gives himself 'a shred of meat, as if to fill the time', eats it, fills his plate and reads Flavia's thoughts: 'Having my luncheon after all!' (26). What the reader reads is Cassius's anxiety about his first wife's return, his uneasiness with his second wife, and his insecurity. The elder Mr Clare's calm humour, Flavia's common sense and Cassius's weak self-serving are contrasted in domestic routines which are charged with meanings: the carving, the meat, the serving, the rhythm and community of the daily meal come to be recognised as metonyms by Cassius's troubled imagination and the reader. Through violations, the scene shows the need for ceremony, recalling Lear's sane answer to Regan's callous utilitarianism, 'Reason not the need.' Cassius's crazy suggestion of abolishing meals comes from his deep fear that the harmony of marriage, the ordered family, and his role as head of the house are in danger. At a later breakfast, after a fake suicide, he repeats the indulgent abstention of the food-martyrs, Sophia and Josephine, answering Flavia's offer of more coffee by indicating 'the full cup at his elbow', telling Ainger, the butler, that he has not touched his food, which 'need not be wasted', and turning his head 'from side to side' at the offer of fresh toast (154–5). Asked if he is not himself, he gives a rather good answer, 'We are all too much ourselves at breakfast' (157). Eventually, he asks '"Well, is breakfast at an end?" . . . seeming to chance to push his full cup into view', and his wife observes, 'Breakfast has not begun for Cassius' (159). He is putting on an act but probably not hungry, as he goes from the breakfast table to the library, where he is found unconscious, this time from a fatal heart attack.

In *Mother and Son*, there is a pattern of significant meals as characters shuttle between two large comfortable houses, and relationships shift with each visit. There is a full representation of host and guest roles, without commentary. We begin with tea laid out for Miss Burke to consume alone after an unsuccessful interview for post as companion, and we are told that she has bread and butter and plain cake. Hester Wolsey, the next applicant, is more successful, and she performs in a scene where tea is ceremonially provided, though not served, by the tyrannical Miranda's son, Rosebery, who re-positions table and chairs, and confesses a reluctance to tell his mother he no longer likes sugar in tea. Miranda comes in, suspiciously interpreting re-arranged furniture and empty tea-pot, but manages to welcome the newcomer, who turns Miranda into good host by cunningly performing as good guest.

Emma Greatheart and the rejected Miss Burke, who becomes Emma's housekeeper, plan luncheon for Miranda, Rosebery and Hester, and after Miranda's death, for her widower, Julius, and Rosebery and Hester. Miss

Burke's coffee and her food, 'good and plentiful and in season' (79), surprise Miranda: 'You are a very good cook, Miss Burke' and 'This is excellently made . . . I regard cooking of this standard on this level as an accomplishment' (84–5). Miranda is a bad hostess but good guest – 'This is a very pleasant house' – though she condescends, 'It is larger than I had imagined' (82), and is surprised that the family dines late.

For a second Greatheart luncheon, after Miranda's death, Emma and Miss Burke plan a simple menu, with better wine than they had at the first luncheon, where the only male guest was Rosebery. Emma expects to use better china than the everyday kind but when Miss Burke says it is 'cracked and mended. But . . . old and good . . . rather rare', she repeats the words with relish. They use the rare china but a 'new and ordinary' table-cloth and newish table-napkins which do not need mending, because they have no 'fine old linen carefully darned' (80), and Miss Burke prefers cooking to sewing. They will be 'like other people' (79) in showing off for guests but do not want to be like them because they really are not like them; the dialogue is a dry, nuanced double-take on being snobbish about being snobbish, social analysis as lively as it is shrewd. When Julius talks to Emma and Rosebery to Miss Burke, Hester breaks up the dialogues because she has her eye on Julius and beneath the brittle surface of domestic ritual and routine runs the Oedipal drama, presence and absence of mother, absence and presence of father, son's attempts to grow up and woo and extricate himself from his mother, before and after her death. The surface breaks at the return party, where Julius and Rosebery propose to Emma and Miss Burke, and Hester reveals her designs on Julius and violates ceremony by letting the family skeletons out of the cupboard, but in the end we are restored to happy housekeeping in the Greatheart household, all women except for Plautus, the tom-cat.

A Father and His Fate stages another tragi-comic drama at afternoon tea, with accessories of tea-pot, cups, saucers, tea, sugar, milk and boiling water, and a struggle for seating, all to reveal deep trouble. This tea ceremony begins as Miles shows his solicitude for his wife, returned from supposed death in time to prevent his deliberated bigamous marriage to the attractive Verena, now married to Malcolm, the nephew and heir. When Ursula tries to explain Verena's power to her mother, she says she 'knows how to serve herself' (155), and the metaphor is appropriate. Wife and ex-fiancée meet at the tea-table, where Verena served but must now be served. The routines and objects of tea-time accumulate innuendo:

'Ellen, my dear, that silver teapot is heavy for you. Could Ursula manage it?'

'I suppose she did, when I was away. And I did before I went. And I am still equal to it.'

'I remember you thought I should not be,' said Verena to Miles. 'It needs a stronger wrist than mine.' (159)

And:

'How do you like your tea, Verena?' said Constance, 'My mother is waiting to know.'

'Your father could have told her.'

'I think you can tell her yourself,' said Ellen, smiling.

'I'm not used to saying that sort of thing in this house.'

'I think you must tell me this once. It can be the first and last time.'

Verena made no answer and looked at Miles.

'Oh, I do not know,' he said, withdrawing his eyes. 'It is not the kind of thing I remember.'

'I think you do know.'

Miles seemed not to hear, and looked again at his wife.

'Malcolm, relieve your sister of that teapot. It is too much for her.' (160)

Verena has been the hostess-in-waiting, in the wife's place in more ways than one, and struggles against Ellen's patient, firm resumption of her roles. But re-enactments failing, Verena must concede, 'Well, am I to have any tea?' and 'Oh, let me have it anyhow,' and Ellen fills the cup, passing 'milk and sugar with it'. Verena tries to make defeat victory: '"Now you remember how I have it" . . . taking a very little of each and looking at Miles', but he has chosen: 'Ellen, my dear, your own cup came late. It could not have been a good one. We will ring for some more tea' (163). We focus on every detail as the scene is prolonged, over six pages. Everyday objects are magnified and trivial routines set in slow motion, made strange for one more drama of jealousy and power.

The Mighty and Their Fall briefly returns to the class question of a governess and her appetite, though Miss Starkie and her pupils are more composed than Miss Bunyan and Muriel in *Daughters and Sons*, one less vulnerable and others more sensible. We begin with the children joking about the governess not wanting to wait for lunch, and when their elder brother asks, 'What is the jest?', their grown-up sister says, 'Something about her thinking of food' and he replies, 'I used to be surprised that she did. It seemed to reduce her to our level.' Miss Starkie is easy: 'Well, I feel just about on a line with it at the moment . . . So I have come down to pursue it, as no-one came up to me. I suppose you are to have your share downstairs today.' When asked, 'Were you assailed by pangs of hunger?', she is unperturbed: 'Well, by something milder than those' (5–6). Agnes makes conversation at table – 'It is a change to have luncheon here' – and is rebuked by her brother for showing off – 'You say things for people to hear them' – but tyrannical grandmother Selina orders silence (7–8). There is another fat episode: asked 'Are you leaving that on your plate . . .?', Leah replies, 'Yes. Only an animal could eat it' (10).

In *The Last and the First*, we return to a sustained pattern of expressive meals, starting with breakfast and a familiar argument between Eliza and Hermia, stepmother and stepdaughter, whose relationship gives the book's title and theme:

> 'Hermia, do you eat no fat at all?'
> 'None, as you know. I am not a stranger to you.'
> 'Well, you almost are . . . I hardly understand this intensity of feeling over food. It is not such a great matter.'
> 'I might say the same to you. Though we are talking of fat not food.'
> 'Well-behaved people betray no feeling about such things.' (8)

The contentious subject recurs at a neighbour's table, where the slightly more tolerant Jocasta tells her grandson, Osbert, another fat-hater, that he should know 'how to cut a ham': 'You should cut the fat and lean together, and leave what you can't eat.' His sister Erica complains, 'Can't we forget the ham? . . . It dominates the sideboard, but it need hardly do the same to our lives.' Jocasta offers her son, Hamilton, a choice of ham or hot fish, gives her granddaughter, Amy, no choice – 'The fish should be used' – and commends the hacked ham to the butler – 'Some of the fat may have to be cut away', to which he replies, 'standing with his eyes on it', 'Yes, ma'am, to put the edible portion at disposal . . .' (33–7).[10] They look ahead to the next meal, as you do: Jocasta plans to visit Amy's headmistress for tea but Amy fends her off: 'She has her tea taken to her room.' Hamilton says he will not be at luncheon except 'In thought'. When lunch arrives, Jocasta is in one of her moods: 'No words, if you please! We can eat and drink without them,' making Erica murmur, 'So our companionship will be phantom' (37–8).

When Jocasta's grandchildren visit Eliza's house, the entertainment of strangers transforms tyrant to gracious hostess: '[It] is one [of our ways] to go into luncheon at this hour . . . I hope one of yours to do justice to it. Here is my husband, glad to welcome guests and have a full table' (43). There is a less happy party where Miss Murdoch, Hermia's partner in the school, in whose failures the family has invested, is an impossible guest. There are no particulars, just general directions – 'they went to the luncheon table,' 'the occasion wore to its end' (83) – but table-talk is eloquent, the guest's exclamatory, abstract and poetic idiolect perfect for fobbing off the hosts' polite hints:

> 'We are anxious for our daughter to succeed in this venture. I wish I knew there was a chance of it. She is at her best when she has a free hand' . . .
>   'Ah, a free hand, our own way! Do they give it to us, the forces that point our path?' (82)

The choric retrospect is nicely understated: 'I talked to her a little' . . . 'It seemed to be the thing to do. I had no thought of making the most of myself' . . . 'I did the same' . . . and 'We have had enough of her today' (84).

At a school concert, Compton-Burnett goes on observing guests and hosts, in collisions of social and personal relations and the drama of brief encounters. Teachers, pupils and families circulate: 'tea was handed by the girls to the guests, who were uncertain whether it was a grave or a festive occasion, and were not helped to a decision' (55). Jocasta talks tactlessly to Amy's friends about her granddaughter, who, 'although possessed of two personalities . . . had the use of none', and, to Amy's dismay, invites them to tea. Amy feels uneasy 'as members of both her worlds were present' and pretends the 'pendulous' Hamilton is not her uncle (55, 35). The occasion brings about life-changing conversation – as parties do – between Hermia and Hamilton: shortly afterwards he proposes marriage, is rejected, dies and leaves her a fortune. Eliza had more than one reason for nagging about wasted ham-fat, and Hermia rescues her impoverished family as well as bringing about the power-shift signalled in the title.

The minutiae of daily existence come from imagination and experience. The novelist reflects her own appetite and taste as Sabine carves chicken and lamb in *Daughters and Sons* and Emma Greatheart and her housekeeper plan hearty, plain meals in *Mother and Son*, and she reinvents wartime rations and shortages for *Manservant and Maidservant* when Horace Lamb counts chops and doles out stale cake.[11] Her novels contribute to social history, anthropology and biography, but they are works of art. The food and drink and hospitality, lavished or begrudged, is invented and particularised, and the minute detail, concentration and repetition make the meals stranger and larger than life. At times, it seems that everything happens at meals, which mark the day, develop character, defamiliarise ordinary life and embed the sensational plot-happenings in the dailiness of life.

Notes

1. See Barbara Hardy, *The Exposure of Luxury: Radical Themes in Thackeray*.
2. See Barbara Hardy, *The Moral Art of Dickens*.
3. Samuel Taylor Coleridge, *Biographia Literaria*, Chapter 14.
4. Viktor Shklovsky, *Literary Theory: An Anthology*.
5. In *Dolores*, *Men and Wives*, *Parents and Children* and *A God and His Gifts*, there are fewer meals and fewer details of the meals. I have cut many meals and many particulars of meals in the novels I discuss.
6. Burgess has apparently taken an external degree, almost certainly at London University, which the novelist could have known about because she studied at Royal Holloway, a London college. Only Burgess and Bigwell (*Two Worlds and Their Ways*) go to a university other than Oxford or Cambridge.
7. Cicely Grieg, who typed all the novels after *Manservant and Maidservant*, says the novelist was careful with commas: *Ivy Compton-Burnett*, 23.
8. Other amorous gazers are men: Dr Chaucer gazes at his future wife, Hetta (*Daughters and Sons*); Sir Roderick Shelley (*Two Worlds and Their Ways*) and Ridley Cranmer (*Parents and Children*) stare at young girls.
9. Hilary Spurling quotes from a conversation with Barbara Robinson: 'he makes one work too hard for such a small result' (*Secrets of a Woman's Heart*, 222). The remark about hating 'people whose golden bowls are broken' is made by Rachel Hardisty in *Men and Wives* (153), when frivolously lamenting her ageing contemporaries; she is probably quoting *Ecclesiastes* (12: 6), but a sly authorial dig at James may well lie behind the joke.
10. See note 17 to Chapter 1 about the two fat episodes.
11. Spurling, *Secrets of a Woman's Heart*, 184–5.

Chapter 7

Games We Play

Compton-Burnett's people play card-games, board-games, word-games, singing games, charades and chess; they pull crackers, blow bubbles, dress up, tease, mimic, joke, make fun of people and ceremonies, engage in horseplay, burst into song, caper about, read books to themselves or each other, and tell stories. Children are taken for walks, and adults occasionally go on walks, usually gentle strolls on terraces or in gardens, once in *Brothers and Sisters* for a long country walk, and in *Parents and Children* for a picnic with sandwiches. Selina Lovat in *Darkness and Day* has loved horse-riding, Paul Cranmer and some of the male Sullivans in *Parents and Children* hunt and shoot, but no one swims, plays tennis, cricket or football, or does gymnastics. As she uses pastimes and games to reveal character, make plots and explore ideas, the novelist playfully and seriously contributes to the study of Homo Ludens.[1]

There are games in all the novels after *Dolores* but it took some time for the novelist to integrate them organically. *Pastors and Masters* is set in a school but there are no organised games; Burgess takes the boys for a walk and he is said to go out 'sometimes before breakfast to get his exercise . . . Young fellows will be thinking of keeping fit' (11). One boy makes a mild joke about the food – 'Johnson . . . had been observing that it was wise to ask for thankful hearts for such mercies' (7) – and Emily Herrick's talk is full of wit and comic irony lost on most of her listeners. In *Brothers and Sisters*, the family is so dominated by griefs and fears that there is no scope for games, and the high jinks the younger son enjoys in London turn out to be illusory. The Stace children's country walk with friends is not an unmixed pleasure because they need to send a telegram saying they will be late to calm their mother's fears. In *Men and Wives*, Gregory Haslam comments on his father's diversions, 'he is happy, doing such lovely things, shooting and riding and reading prayers' (19), and cheerful, self-deceiving Godfrey is the subject of mild criticism, when he is evasive about getting up at night to look at his sick wife or pretends he knew that her will disinherited him if he remarried. Harriet is an idealistic and depressive wife and mother, whose family can only enjoy frivolous large-scale entertaining while she is in hospital being treated for a breakdown.

Daughters and Sons is the first novel with a young child, the giggling and inquisitive Muriel, and her chief amusement is the unkind observation of what she and her grandmother see as the governess's excessive appetite, but games do not become conspicuous or sophisticated until *Parents and Children*, midpoint in Compton-Burnett's career. In this novel and the six that follow, ending with *Mother and Son* in 1955, we find a development of child characters that brings with it an emphasis on play. In *Parents and Children*, the subject of playing games is developed in comic and serious action. There is a large cast of children: Eleanor and Fulbert Sullivan and their nine offspring live with his parents, and as the theme of parenting is explored, so is the psychology and the morality of play. While children play, so do the adults; their games affect and reflect each other. The eldest sons in their early twenties are not too old to fool about: Daniel comes in leading Graham, deposits him 'in a chair . . . with his hand on his collar' to begin a running zany joke about – but also with – his brother, asking Eleanor if she can bear with him, hoping 'a mother's words may succeed when all else fails' (8–9), wishing he could be broken of his habit of 'eating . . . It is such a primitive habit' (18). Graham never protests, while their *folie à deux* is tolerated by his father and amuses their grandmother, Regan, but makes his fussy sister, Luce, ask if it 'is good for Graham to be teased and made a butt?' She is told not to talk nonsense by their humourless mother, who does not really care: 'I don't suppose it does him much harm. He could stop it if he liked' (12). Sir Jesse grumbles about the cost of his grandsons' Cambridge studies, 'Grinning and chattering like apes and costing like dukes!' (34), though he has his playful moments, singing 'Three good women', playing with his wife's cap, and teasing her about being a young woman.

Joyce in *Ulysses* includes activities usually left out of fiction, like urinating and defecating, and Compton-Burnett includes the trivial nothing-in-particular flow which takes up much of our lives. Of course, her artful joking and bickering also serve the psychological action. Daniel says his foolery covers deep feeling, and though he is half-fooling as he says it, he raises the question of motive and meaning. So does Hope

Cranmer, one of the ironic *raisonneurs*: when she makes Regan laugh in spite of her grief, Hope muses, 'I was really out of spirits. I see why the jesters of old were such sad people. If their profession was cheering people who needed it, it would have been unfeeling not to be' (168). Daniel plays around and makes silly jokes but he and Hope are clever clowns who amuse us, draw attention to the play of conversation and bring a touch of meta-comedy to a comic novel.

The novel uses a split-scene set, and in Chapter 11 we move up from play and banter on the ground floor to antics in the nursery: in bed after a late night, three-year-old Nevill is visited by Honor and Gavin, who run in 'at a halt in their morning toilet, followed by a nursemaid baulked in her intention of completing it' (38). Nevill assumes his self-infantilising charm, saying 'He is tired,' Honor and Gavin leap round the room and Nevill grumbles, 'They shake the room.' When Honor shouts, 'Leap into the air,' Nevill copies her words and wants to join in; their mother arrives, tries to calm them down, tells Nevill not to cover up his face, and he assures her 'He never breathes' (41). It is trivial stuff but amusing, and characters are being created. The articulate Honor describes Nevill as fawning on people, and he is a spoilt youngest child, jealous when Hatton, their nurse, cuddles Honor and calls her 'my baby', and referring to himself as a 'girlie' (205).

Like the meals, the games make realistic and metonymic images. Chapter 3 continues the bad – or not very good – mothering as Eleanor grumbles about the nurse: 'What is wrong with the method?' asks Fulbert ... 'A good many things only a mother would see' ... 'Then we cannot expect Hatton to be aware of them' (59). The children come down for dessert but Eleanor decides it is too late; there is chat about Luce and Daniel changing bedrooms, Daniel goes on with his joke about Graham, Sir Jesse complains, and Nevill comes on 'in the manner of a horse, lifting his feet and head in recognisable imitation' (60). The family squabbles, Luce suggests telling Nevill 'his' story, Honor is sent for a book instead, Eleanor is critical, Nevill reverts to trotting but tries to distinguish pony from horse, Luce reads aloud, and Eleanor goes on being a misery: 'Well, is no one coming to talk to me? ... Why did you all come down?' (60–1). Gavin cries, Eleanor frets, Honor meets her eyes, and big brothers come to the rescue:

Daniel and Graham picked up Honor and carried her round the room. She put her arms round their necks and laughed and shouted in reaction. Eleanor looked on with an indulgent smile, and Gavin with an expectant one. Nevill beat his hands on his sides and moved from foot to foot; and when his brothers took Gavin in Honor's stead, broke into wails and maintained them until they came to himself, when he repulsed them and stood abandoned to his sense that nothing could wipe out what had taken place. When Eleanor and Luce had expostulated in vain, and Regan explained with some success, he raised his arms and allowed himself to be lifted, leaning back in his brothers' arms with an air of convalescence. They tightened their hold and quickened their pace, and he held to their shoulders and accepted this compensation for what he had borne, while Honor watched with bright eyes, and Gavin with a smile of gentle interest. (62)

Eleanor tells the boys to give Gavin a last turn; Eleanor tells Gavin to say 'Thank you' to his brothers, like Honor, and to look at them while he speaks, then blames their upset on the journey. The nurse observes, 'It was best to cry it out, madam, whatever it was,' Nevill agrees in third-person style and resumes the trot, and Eleanor says, 'So you are a horse again. Daniel and Graham, have been your horses, haven't they?' Nevill takes no notice, she suggests trotting 'to say goodbye to father', Nevill ignores her and trots off holding his nurse's hand, and Honor and Gavin kiss their parents and 'frolick' from the room. Regan watches it all with interest, unlike Sir Jesse, who 'seldom noticed children, rather because it did not occur to him to do so, than because he disapproved of the practice' (62–3). It is a family at leisure and nothing much has happened, but the games they play not only record the small pains and pleasures of daily life but also keep character and action on the move.

The way adults – not only parents – play with children tells us every-thing. Just before Fulbert leaves for South America, he runs a race with three of his children, 'deciding that interest and entertainment should remain in his children's memory' (73). His slightly unfocused, gentle sympathy, as he joins in the run and gives prizes to winner and losers, shows him as a good father, while the mother assumes their children love her best, delegates their holidays to nursery staff, and routinely suggests walks or rests or games as cure-alls but does not join in. The youngest children, Honor, Gavin and Nevill, unenthusiastically report the pleasures of sandcastles and beachcombing on their holiday; later on, her children are pleased by the prospect of her leaving to live with a second husband, Ridley Cranmer. When their father is eventually reunited with his family, they agree that having him back makes up for having their mother stay too.

When Fulbert is thought dead in South America, the games played by the prospective stepfather, Ridley, are self-serving, and the one he plays with the children the least harmful, but subtly threatening. On his way to explain to her father-in-law that he wants to marry Eleanor, he plays for time:

'So I am to beard the lion in his den.'
'Grandpa is a big lion,' said Nevill . . . 'He can roar very loud.'
'He can at times,' said Honor, making a mature grimace, and glancing to see if Ridley had had the advantage of it.
'Do you often play in the hall?' said the latter.
'Sometimes when it is wet,' said Gavin.
'Shall I play at lions with you?' said Ridley, looking at a skin on the floor, and seeming to be struck by an idea that would serve his own purpose. (232)

Inspired by the need to procrastinate, his own metaphor and the rug, he invents the game while Nevill retreats to 'a secure height' on the staircase:

Ridley put the skin over his head and ran in different directions, uttering threatening sounds and causing Honor and Gavin to leap aside with cries of joy and mirth. Nevill watched the action with bright, dilated eyes, and, when Ridley ran in his direction, fled farther upstairs with piercing shrieks. Hatton descended in expostulation, and Miss Mitford in alarm, the latter not having distinguished between the notes of real and pleasurable terror in Nevill's voice. (232)

Of course, it is the kind of rough game adults may play lovingly and innocently with children, and we have seen the happy horseplay in the dining-room, but these antics are neither loving nor innocent. There is no heavy symbolism but everything is expressive: playfulness, carelessness, attempt to ingratiate, high excitement and a touch of sadism. Neither characters nor reader yet know exactly how the game carries a threat. The novelist stays cool as she prepares her future action – and exhibits the high tension and destructive element in some of the games we play.

In Chapter 6, there is a discussion of games in the school-room when the boys show their new toys, a bow they have made and arrows they have bought – weapons ingratiatingly suggested by the new and insecure governess, Miss Pilgrim – and they shock goody-goody Faith Cranmer, whose quotation, 'A robin redbreast in a cage', shows the novelist wickedly using Blake for satire, pointing the difference between deep, humane compassion and sanctimonious parade. (Faith's stepmother, Hope, does the opposite earlier when she adapts a sad line from Tennyson's 'Break, Break, Break', 'the echo of a voice that is still', in her running joke about her predecessor, the first Mrs Cranmer [108].) Honor does not help by literal-mindedly reassuring Faith that 'Father kills other birds' so they need not kill robins, nor Nevill by promising to shoot a little bird for her, as she kisses him goodbye (177). Faith's weakness for him is almost a redeeming touch, but these children are infallible judges of the adult world, and after she intrusively condoles with them on their father's supposed death, Faith is coolly described by Honor as 'Not a high type' (216). Nevill plans to hold a funeral and say prayers for the birds they destroy, like his equally charming and destructive successor, Toby, in *The Present and the Past*. The children quote their father's blood sports as support, mentioning his birds that 'All hang down' (177), and earlier, in Chapter 4, the Cranmer and Sullivan men have discussed the ethics and pleasures of fox-hunting. Neither the children nor the child-lovers are there to touch our hearts.

Of course, the games can be well intentioned and beneficial. Regan, the grandmother, is lovingly playful and serious as she comforts Henry with her allegorical story about a bird returning to its fledglings.[2] Mullet, the nursery-maid, amuses the children and herself with her spontaneous fantasies, truly inspired when she transforms Eleanor's engagement to Ridley into the tale of a sinister, scar-faced stranger, which rivets Gavin and amuses the more sceptical Honor. Hatton, the loved and loving nurse, scarcely has time to play, but there is an affectionate playful touch in her stock reply when asked her age: 'Older than you but not a hundred' (40). Humourless, unimaginative Eleanor never plays with her children and her nearest approach to joining in a game is her unconvincing 'So you are a horse again' (63), where the tone is what has come to be called patronising. She is not an entirely unsympathetic character, but unusual as a mother in fiction in finding her role so uncongenial that she has to make conversation with her own small children.

The double anagnorisis or recognition scene in Chapter 11 is precipitated by Ridley's false and patronising ways. Thwarted by Fulbert's return, he pretends composure and sits down. Nevill is confused about the return of his real father after being prepared for a stepfather, and climbs on Ridley's knee, when 'holding to his line of playing a normal part'; the trusted guardian asks rashly and playfully, 'Now I must see what I can find in my pockets . . . Here is a purse and a notebook and a cigar case, and a gold pencil case with lead in it' (284). He laughs on the other side of his face when Gavin finds an incriminating loose leaf in the notebook, and in one stroke proves he can read grown-up writing and reveals Ridley's duplicity and planned bigamy, though the deceiver takes his revenge by exposing Sir Jesse's double life.

The mystery and consequences of that secret past have already been presented in the sub-plot, which also makes its subdued contribution to the theme of leisure and amusement: a rent-free cottage in the grounds shelters Sir Jesse's three illegitimate children, who are quiet, charming intellectuals – a teacher, a writer who publishes but does not earn much, and a stay-at-home. They do not discover their parentage until the end of the novel, and it is not going to change anything. Their pastimes are valued as respite, holiday and reunion; they enjoy their own company, friends who drop in for a chat, and what they treasure above all, 'Books and a fire' (148).

Elders and Betters features the most elaborate and original children's game, the imitation of religious ritual, confession and prayer by Julius and Theodora, who invent a private religion and worship the gods Chung and Sung-Li – they observe that 'Sung' is like but not too like 'Son'. They know it will have to be given up at puberty and exchanged for the conventional religion, but meantime enjoy the combination of fun and serious confession – the latter is needed because their amusements include pilfering small change and books. Their cousin, Reuben, is allowed to attend as an occasional acolyte, but excluded at the final great ceremony after their mother's death, here emphasising that special childhood pang of being left out, in a reminder that religious sects, as well as children's games, have dangerous and aggressive features.

In *Manservant and Maidservant*, Marcus experiments with the science of freezing and the magic of images; Jasper is an amateur carpenter, who makes wooden boxes for the joy of his craft; and all the children like reading or being read to. Marcus's games are part of plot and character. His test is pointedly made in the icy school-room, where the temperature is controlled by Horace, who makes his children exercise and drill to save heating, leading them round the room; and when he has left, Marcus melts, moulds and pricks a candle in his father's likeness for a sympathetic magic, which gives Horace instant rheumatic pains. The children do get Christmas presents: writing-desks, writing materials and books. The motherly eldest sister, Sarah, reads her present, *Lamb's Tales from Shakespeare*, to the younger ones, but only nine-year-old Avery is allowed a Christmas stocking, and he is persuaded to accept Jasper's best box for the partly eaten bag of sweets from his unpacked, repacked and unpacked-again stocking. Avery is afraid of crackers, but after Sarah fails in her plan to take his cracker upstairs, he is forced to pull them by Horace in seasonably hearty mood, and Avery brings the cheap cracker-toys to join the father's reading of the Christmas story, postponed when two children get the giggles. When Avery is discovered stealing sweets, he is terrified by his father to the point of nightmare, and his siblings do their best to distract him with play:

> Sarah was seated on Avery's bed, reading from the Book of Job, not from any sense of fitness, but because it was her brother's choice. He lay with a convalescent air, his face responding as the words confirmed his memory. Tamasin blew soap bubbles, that he broke with a languid hand, and his brothers performed a series of antics, looking to see if he were attentive and entertained. (66)

Two Worlds and Their Way is in part a school-story, but there are no school games, though there is some aggressive and funny interrogation when Sefton meets the other new boys:

> 'Then has your father more than one wife?'
>   'No, of course not. The first wife has to die before a man can have a second . . .'
>   'Then your father does not keep a harem?'
>   'Of course not . . . Oliver's mother died and he married again later.'
>   'But she was still his wife. So is your mother his concubine?'
>   'No, of course not . . .'
>   . . . 'We want to get at the truth . . . Perhaps his father is a Mohammedan.' (153–4)

The bewildered and harried Sefton is reduced to tears but the boys keep up the joke with informed literary allusion: 'Well there is no need to cry . . . Your father may love your mother the best. That does happen with concubines. I daresay Agamemnon loved Cassandra better than Clytemnestra' (155). They bait the matron about the school rules, pretending to misunderstand phrases like 'Observe silence', 'Observe punctuality' and 'Keep punctuality', and quibbling about the difference between unpacking in the dormitory and visiting it, as Compton-Burnett adapts her interest in the use of words and destructive play to the school-boy sense of humour. The girls in Clemence's school are aggressive but less amusing: as a new girl Clemence is driven to prevaricate and lie by catty interrogations about hair-style, clothes and servants, but she enjoys the friendly fun of walking in a linked row, and 'the break-up party' – presented only in prospect and retrospect – is 'a sight you would not believe' . . . 'eighty girls . . . You should have seen them going downstairs in their party clothes!' (214).

There is enjoyable clandestine mime and acting in the home world, with star performances from Aldom, the butler, Sir Roderick's illegitimate son, who has 'two characters, of which one was his own. Whether or no he was a prince in disguise downstairs, he was someone in disguise' (28). He is a quick-change artist, switching plot, scene and role in a flash when authority interrupts:

> 'Aldom, do the scene at the inn, when you fetched your father from the supper' . . .
>
> 'And not too many of the words, with Miss Clemence here . . . She won't have to get used to what you had to' . . .
>
> The children stood, absorbed in the scene . . . It held its own until it seemed to sustain a sudden shock. A change seemed to shiver through it. The innkeeper spoke with another voice, lived and moved as another man . . .
>
> 'A scene from the village school?' said Maria. 'What a life-like master!' . . .
>
> 'They had heard some talk about school, my lady,' said Adela, in bustling explanation . . . 'And Aldom is something of a mimic and was a character when he was at school.' (39)

After Maria has left, '"Mother might have heard the drunken talk," said Sefton, in an awed tone' (41), and when we eventually find out why the butler has blue eyes like Sir Roderick's, we may reflect on that drunken father: here and elsewhere, Compton-Burnett's jigsaw of secret lives has small, significant pieces we place when we come to the end of the novel or re-read it. Not for this novelist the Victorian tying up of loose ends on the last page.

Aldom's second impressive performance, also interrupted, mocks and mimics Lesbia, Sir Roderick's sister-in-law, who runs a girls' school. It is accidentally witnessed by the victim, who manages a dry self-reassurance – 'I have lost no time in implanting an impression of my personality' – but betrays her discomposure to the reader by restraining an involuntary gesture, a tribute to the finesse of costume and props:

> Miss Petticott, her pupils and Adela sat at attention before a masquerading figure. The trappings of the latter sorted themselves out to

the eye. The stuffing of Adela's armchair supplied the short grey hair; a scarf of Miss Petticott's the grey and shadowy garment; a strap, with some scissors depending, the belt with its silver attachment, at sight of which Lesbia restrained a movement of her hand towards her waist. (61–2)

The performer calmly disrobes and, asked if he has nothing better to do, turns excuse to accusation: 'Well, Sir Roderick, I have acted at school before, as is known to her ladyship, it not being the custom to work from morning till night. And this time it seemed to fit the occasion, as it was an imminent experience' (62). Lesbia gets in a jab at the flustered governess, whom she looks down on – 'And it has its educational value, Miss Petticott?'; Maria is impressed by Aldom's quick move from observation to imitation; Sir Roderick cannot stop laughing; and Lesbia calls him childish and condescends in pedantic style, 'And very realistic it all was. Observed and plausible and failing in none of the stock humours' (63). The implications of Aldom's mimicry – though no word or gesture is specified – stay with us as Lesbia plays an increasingly antipathetic part in the story, authoritarian, insensitive, mercenary, impermeable to criticism and dreadful with children.

In *Darkness and Day*, children's games get rougher: Rose and Viola resist their self-appointed governess, Mildred, by insisting on painting, then do a deal, agreeing to begin with art and move on to dictation and arithmetic. Throughout their four brief scenes together, they all play with words, aggressively and defensively:

> 'Are you painting?' she said, in a tone of pleasant interest.
> 'Well, you can see we are,' said Rose.
> 'Yes, I can. It was a useless question, wasn't it?'
> 'Yes, it was.'
> 'But I am afraid painting is not lessons.'
> 'Of course it is not, or we shouldn't have been doing it before you came.' (121–2)

By the second lesson, Mildred (though only Mildred) knows they are half-sisters but the word-game stays the same, a literal-minded refusal by the children to accept the loose language of phatic communion, played for different reasons and in different moods by the adults in most of the books, here for what the children call war between natural enemies:

'So you are settled and busy,' she said.

There was no reply.

'Is neither of you going to say good-morning to me?'

'You didn't say it to us,' said Rose.

'I did not use the words. But that does not matter. It is usual to say something pleasant on meeting in the morning.'

'Why was that pleasant?' said Viola.

'Well, I will try to do better. Good morning to you both.' (165)

The formidable children may horrify readers but Mildred is patronising, a bad teacher and slow to learn. Outside lessons, Rose and Viola can keep the peace. They love having tea in the kitchen but their main amusement is story-books: Rose, the bookworm, rushes to the shelves the moment they go into the nursery and Viola fears she will never speak to her but is told there are books for young children too. Rose keeps a book under her pillow to read if Viola wakes up and has the light on; she reads *The Old Curiosity Shop* and either this or another Dickens novel – it is not clear – is used to learn words for dictation during a brief school-room truce.[3] Viola has read Bunyan but does not want to see or remember the picture of Giant Despair and Rose has read about Oedipus in *The Book of Legends*. The love of books is used for the plot: Rose overhears her parents' talk about incest and innocently spreads the rumour; we get a first hint of Mrs Spruce's relationship to the girls when she tells them a story about the old and the new houseboys.

In *The Present and the Past*, games are more prominent; there is not much fun for the children, but Toby enjoys throwing his plate on the floor, seeing it broken into bits by his siblings, and graduates to smash a vase – more broken bowls. The best game is serious pleasure, the funeral of a dead mole, for which Megan writes an elegy[4] and Toby officiates with an impressively informed address: 'Dearly beloved brethren. Let us pray. Ashes and ashes. Dust and dust. This is our brother. Poor little mole! Until he rise again!' 'Why, you will make a proper parson, sir,' says William, who compares Toby to his actor-uncle with whom the humourless Cassius has quarrelled (44). Funeral echoes return in sleepy murmur and bedtime tantrums: 'But very nice box and wake up again to-morrow . . . Bennet give Toby some first. Not Megan; Toby!' (51). Grown-ups act as well as children, and the plot hinges on Cassius's fake overdose and his unnecessary death when heart failure is mistaken for another fake suicide in the risky game of 'Crying Wolf'. In these novels, as in life, games are serious and life is often a game.

This is true in *Mother and Son* when a game brings on a doubled climax. Rosebery and Julius have just got engaged to Emma Greatheart and her housekeeper, Miss Burke, and they are discussing their futures when Emma's former companion Hester makes a formal entrance with the teenage children she is looking after:

> The door opened and a start went through the group. A change came into the room. Hester and the children entered, smiling and conscious, carrying some clothes they used for charades.
>
> 'Now we have a surprise for you,' said Hester. 'There is a play for you to see. Alice has written it, and Francis arranged it for us. We are the harmless, necessary actors, and you are the equally indispensable audience.'
>
> 'Miss Wolsey,' said Rosebery, moving forward, 'we also have a play to present, a play that has its action in real life. It may interest you the more for that. You see us as we stand. It is thus that we shall take our parts on the stage of life.'
>
> Hester looked swiftly from one pair to another.
>
> 'A modern farce is it? A mating in the approved mock way? Suitable because it is the opposite. Well, it will serve its purpose. We must see one play after the other, and judge between them. I am inclined to back the children's.'
>
> 'Miss Wolsey, we will see your play indeed. It will make a celebration for us on this day of our lives.' (174)

There is a break in ceremony as life goes one better than art. Prologue is not followed by the rehearsed performance and the audience takes the stage. Like *Lovers' Vows* in Austen's *Mansfield Park*, Hester's charade is never performed. After her formal solemn speech, she breaks out in jealous rage because she has hoped to marry Julius, not celebrate his marriage to her friend, and spitefully reveals the family secrets: the niece and nephews, Alice, Francis and Adrian, are Julius's illegitimate children, Rosebery his wife's son by another man. It is a neat reversal of fortune, role and mood, and a clash of game and reality which serves character and plot with double climax and several surprises. And we never know what the charade would have been.

The novel ends with a less dramatic game: earlier in the book, Rosebery has taught Francis and Adrian a game of cards, and we return to it at the very end, when Julius and Rosebery have been jilted, and are at a loose end.

'Father, will you join us in a game of cards?' said Rosebery, drawing out
a chair . . .
'Will nothing else absorb Rosebery's energy?' murmured Francis. 'If
only Aunt Miranda were alive!'
'Francis, that will be the epitome of my life.'
'Would she have liked us to play cards?' said Adrian.
'Was it that doubt, that prevented your playing? . . . I can relieve you
of it. She taught me to play herself, when I was a boy.'
'And now has left him partnerless,' murmured Francis.
'And now has left me as you say, Francis,' said Rosebery. (208)

The conclusion is a drily comic anti-climax, a little relaxation to pass
the time after all the secrets, scandals, blighted romances and reversals,
with Rosebery, the partnerless mother's boy, gently teased as he fondly
remembers his mother, Miranda, who was so far from playful.

In *A God and His Gifts*, the theme of a destructive creator is mir-
rored in three-year-old charmer Henry, who breaks the toy horse given
him by his adoring adoptive father – actually his real one – mimics his
grandfather with stick and spectacles, and tears up his drawing in creative rage. Games and pastimes are more heavily symbolic when happy
grandparents, grandchildren and reluctant butler join in 'Ring a Ring a
Roses' and 'Here We Come Gathering Nuts in May', where the deceived
wife Ada is cast as victim, the point made clearer by local variation: 'We
will have Ada for Nuts in May . . . We will send Hereward to fetch her
away . . .' They 'engage in the contest'; Hereward wins and Ada weeps.
The eldest son, Merton, says, 'I knew it was not a game. It was the
opposite of one,' and Ada concludes portentously, 'It has done its work.
It has shown us things as they have to be, as we must see they are' (45).
The scene ends with the gambolling grandfather 'expressing goodwill
to everyone', improvising more variations about 'A touch of frost in the
nuts in May' which 'we managed to smooth . . . away,' to conclude, 'Oh,
there you all are! How that jingle sounds in one's head! The tune that
is, of course. The words have no meaning,' to make his daughter ask,
in another touch of meta-play, 'Can that ever be said of words?' (46).

In *The Last and the First*, the book left unfinished, there is a scene,
important to plot, where family and guests play a kind of 'Consequences',
a word-game where each player writes one line of 'any poem in print' to
accumulate nonsense or accidental sense. The game is announced with
a mock-solemn quotation from Cowper's 'Retirement', 'The want of
occupation is not rest / A mind that's vacant is a mind distressed', by the
second daughter Madeline, who substitutes 'The want' for the correct

and metrically subtler 'Absence'. We never see the group effort, only the fuss and protest and commentary: 'People are always serious about games,' 'We don't play to win' and 'But it is when people win that they feel pleasure' (125). The poem is read aloud by the household tyrant, Eliza, who 'rendered the lines with justice both to them and to herself, making what she could of their lack of relation'; there is 'some spontaneous mirth, a renewal of it that was less spontaneous, and a silence that perhaps had the best claim to the word' (126). The announcement of another game and the need for more paper is frustrated by players who have torn up their paper, scribbled on it, lost it, given it away or made it into a hat, and in the end by the crucial discovery of a purloined letter. It is a convincing little representation of the boredom and bother that party games can involve, and serves the plot.

Compton-Burnett never presents the game as a big central event with a structure of its own, like the amateur production of *Lovers' Vows* in *Mansfield Park*, the charades in *Jane Eyre*, or the *Winter's Tale* tableau in *Daniel Deronda*, though, like these famous examples, her games now and then parallel or symbolise features in the novel itself. She is not interested in the culture and history of games, which interested Johan Huizinga, or games as part of the learning process, which interested psychologists like Jean Piaget, but as a cool and comic novelist with her own experience of tricks and *jeux d'esprit*. Unlike Huizinga, she shows game-playing as socially and psychologically inseparable from other aspects of daily life. She recognises the art in the games we all play, with an awareness reflected in the shared imagistic vocabulary of pastime and art, like 'play' and 'players', but she has a special interest, implicit and explicit, in language games and, of course, her favourite is conversation. She is aware of the fun, complicity, relaxation, dangers and destructiveness of games – games which range from family banter to blood sports, amuse or distract or distress babies and adults, stimulate serious debate, exercise our brain, amuse and entertain us, waste and kill time.

Notes

1. The key text is Johan Huizinga's *Homo Ludens*, but he excludes domestically assimilated games like those in Compton-Burnett. The aggressive element or origin is often explicit or implicit in her games, but she also shows play at its most purely playful.
2. I return to this episode in Chapter 10.

3. There is one word, 'metamorphosis', which they cannot read because the book is torn; they consult their nurse and the servants about it, but this seems to be a careless slip on Compton-Burnett's part since the word does not appear to be in any of Dickens's novels or Christmas stories.
4. I discuss this more fully in Chapter 8.

Chapter 8

Books We Read and Write

There are really no other arts in the novels apart from literature. Sir Jesse in *Parents and Children* is given to bursts of song, there is hymn-singing by cook and butler in *Manservant and Maidservant*, and a piano-teacher in *Two Worlds and Their Ways*,[1] family portraits in several novels, and a mention of Dutch portraiture in *Darkness and Day*, but the novels are full of allusion to fiction, plays and poetry. Compton-Burnett was well read in drama and literature, especially the English classics, and the Greek and Latin studied for her degree, and in *Mother and Son* there is a cat called Plautus after the Roman dramatist. She liked theatre, which influenced her, though she insisted that her conversation novels were unlike plays.[2] Elizabeth Taylor wrote to Liddell about going with her to the Royal Court to see *Happy Days*, which she enjoyed,[3] and it is good to think of her as liking Beckett, whose bleak, stoical irony has much in common with hers, though it is a long way from her drawing-rooms to his dustbins. She admired Jane Austen, a touchstone in two or three of her novels, though she dismissed the idea of direct influence.[4] She named characters arbitrarily or playfully after famous writers or their dramatis personae: for instance, Donne, Bunyan, Shelley, Chaucer, Swift, Edgeworth, Jocasta, Regan and Miranda. There is one character who is a great dramatist, children who write poetry, three successful novelists, several unpublished writers in various genres, and a few rapidly dismissed scholars. The allusions to English writing and classical literature are all mediated through responses of individual readers.

A portrait of an artist first appears in *Dolores* but when Compton-Burnett found her distinctive style after the war, she did all she could to suppress it.[5] This may have encouraged critics who saw a poor imitation of George Eliot in authorial narrator, funeral scene and the subject of self-sacrifice. *Dolores* is an odd book, with a dutiful heroine, family drama, eccentric doctors and clergymen, two austerely dialogic scenes in a woman's college, and the grotesque genius, Sigismund Claverhouse, who is like nothing else in her work or anyone else's.

Claverhouse is the best thing in *Dolores* but interesting only in isolated episodes. His love for Dolores's fellow-student, Perdita, their marriage and her tragic diary are barely shown but views on his art are presented in some detail. In the discussion of George Eliot's influence, Casaubon has been cited as a model, but all the sterile scholar has in common with Compton-Burnett's dramatist is an aged, unattractive body and a bad marriage. *Dolores* is a bad novel but it does attempt to say something about the literary imagination which is interesting in its own right, and obliquely reflexive. The genius in the novel thinks about his dramatic art, and takes a passionate pride in it.

Claverhouse reads his mother and his friend, Soulsby, his new play, which Soulsby calls 'wonderful', 'great' and 'marvellously deep', provoking the dramatist to reflect:

'Deep? . . . Yes, it is deep. There is no great play that is not deep. But there are great plays that are not true. Mine is true, if you could but know it . . .
. . . Listen! When Althea hears that her father is dead, she utters no sound, no word – that is true. The madman in his lucid days thinks more of the life he shares for the time with his kind, than of the certain madness before him – that is true. When the teacher is enfeebled beyond the toil of his years, his thoughts are of the pupils whom he taught in his prime, rather than those he is yielding up with their present gratitude. When old Jannetta is failing, she is cold to the friends who tend her age, and yearns towards her kin of blood.' (133)

His friend agrees – 'Yes, yes . . . I see that it is true—that all—that all your plays are true' – but Claverhouse protests, 'that is not what I said . . . In all of them there is truth; but the two last are all true' (133). The emphasis on truth is striking in the first work of a novelist so concerned with truth, both in her characters' self-scrutinising conversation, and in her art, which places psychological honesty higher than charming, flattering or comforting the reader.

The intense discussion follows Claverhouse's reading his play with 'the reader's voice, under the veil of its own qualities . . . the voice of each character' (130). Dialogue between writer and critic is artfully elliptical, dropping us into an excited discussion, with the play's themes of family, teaching, madness, age and time sufficiently specified for intimate, allusive, literary talk where much can be taken for granted.

We do not know precisely what Claverhouse is talking about – title and plot, verse or prose, for audience or reader – but we know the writer's feelings as he reflects on his work and finds it good. It is not all creative delight; life is short, art is hard, and though he first dismisses Soulsby's objection to an inappropriate opening and some superficial 'inelegances' as pedantic quibbling, later on he says he is grateful and loses himself in creative revision.

He talks to Dolores about his work in a tutorial, after he discovers that she knows his plays, and what he says is brief and generalised, charged with the strong feeling of the writer who is teaching, mediated through an impressionable student:

> It was not in chief his own plays that he taught, but, as he told her in a moment of emotion, 'the greatest thing that life offered to men'—the study of men, as shown in nature, and, as grasped from nature, in the plays of the greatest dramatists of different time and race; in whom, with a natural dignity which thrilled her to passion, he numbered himself: and at times he demanded not only understanding of these, but studies of character from her own pen. (143)

It is a fine humanist claim for art, and for teaching literature. The teaching method is like that of Charlotte Brontë's tutor, Constantin Héger, whose *devoirs* involved reading and imitating character sketches of famous men; Compton-Burnett would not have known about them, but it is possible that in school or university she was set the kind of exercise so important in the creative and sentimental education of the earlier novelist. In any case, she admired Charlotte, thinking her better than Emily, and read about pupil–master relationships and *devoirs* in *The Professor*, *Villette* and *Shirley*. She never made such grand, ambitious claims for herself, or for the other fictitious writers in her novels, but her insistence on telling truths 'as shown in nature, and as grasped from nature' is illustrated and scrutinised by many characters, in a conspicuously dramatic form. The art for which Claverhouse makes such large claims is drama, his model probably the closet drama practised in the latter half of the nineteenth century, but the significance of what he says goes beyond his genre. Compton-Burnett was never again to imagine an artist's imagination so ambitiously, so passionately and so seriously. And her choice of a dramatist anticipates her own conspicuously dramatic fiction.

Her only other real portrait of the artist comes forty-two years later in

The Present and the Past, and it is subdued and quiet. The most prominent and complex character in this novel is no artist but the insensitive
Cassius Clare. He fails in all his personal relations except those with his
father and the butler but he is not completely unsympathetic, and one
of his sons says after he dies, 'I think he loved us more than he seemed
to' (178). He wants to be loved but is no good at loving. We see him
with his seven-year-old daughter, Megan, when he reads her epitaph for
a dead mole, printed on a bit of cardboard:

> 'My name is Mole.
> I lie here buried deep.
> I rest beneath this scroll
> And fold my hands in everlasting sleep.' (45–6)

Cassius asks at once, 'Who wrote that?', clearly judging the poem as professional; his next response, 'Who helped you?', still sounds impressed;
finally, after carping, questioning and re-reading, he triumphantly spots
plagiarism.

> 'My name is Joy,' said Cassius, frowning to himself, 'I seem to remember
> something of the kind, something by some poet.'
>   'Megan was not copying anything,' said Guy, 'She wrote the poem
> out of her head.'
>   'Ah, ha!' said his father, 'So it was out of someone else's, and I daresay
> the better for that, I thought it was rather professional somehow.' (47)

Megan's elegy joins the small group of real poems by fictitious characters, including Stephen's villanelle in *A Portrait of the Artist as a Young
Man* and the Quetzalcoatl poems in Lawrence's *The Plumed Serpent.*
Cassius Clare is called after a poet, and though he boasts about his reading and literary memory, while unwilling to recognise his daughter's
talent, his grudging response is a kind of praise. Moreover, the poem
gets unequivocal praise from everyone else. Megan's half-brother, Guy,
reveals that he is a poet when he replies to Cassius's snide question,
'And are you a poet?', by saying he is but 'not as good a one as Megan'.
Guy's stepmother and Megan's mother, Flavia, says if there is an echo it
is probably unconscious, and anyway 'a small thing', and the intelligent
governess, Miss Ridley, says excellent things about the poem and the
value of art: the poem is 'at once true and imaginative', 'work', 'of use'
and 'something that exists outside yourself . . . a great thing to feel' (48).

What Cassius half-recalls as 'My name is Joy', or 'something of the kind', is the conversation-poem 'Infant Joy', from Blake's *Songs of Innocence* – 'I have no name / I am but two days old / What shall I call thee? / I happy am / Joy is my name' – and its innocent elation makes a contrast and a parallel with the compassion which inspired Megan. There is not much joy for the children in this novel, which begins with pity for a dying hen being pecked by its fellows, and resounds with Guy's melancholy refrain, 'Oh dear, oh dear!' Blake's lyric is a loving exchange between a baby and parent, an ironic reflection on Cassius, who finds parenting hard; Flavia, who tries to treat her children and stepchildren equally; and Catherine, who has been wretchedly separated from her sons for nine years.

The poem develops character, intensifies feeling and pays tribute to creativity. Miss Ridley calls it true as well as imaginative, clearly responding to the fine detail of the folded hands, and the mole's aware-ness of burial. When Megan first saw the mole, she said, 'It has real hands,' and what impressed her is re-imagined in the hands folded in piety. When the mole is made to speak of deep burial, we recall the earth in which it lived and moved. Tact and delicacy keep image and idea within the bounds of a child's knowledge and imagination – to think otherwise is to think with Cassius, who is triumphantly ungenerous. Of course, the poem was not written by a child but by an adult imaginative enough to write a poem a child might have written. (And a writer who had read Blake.) It is a portrait of an artist. There are several young and old poets in the novels, but only one other fictitious poem is mentioned. It is written by the novelist, Hereward Egerton, in *A God and His Gifts,* to a woman he loved, inscribed to her in a book, never published, read by several characters but not quoted.

The first professional writer is Claverhouse; the next two are John Ponsonby and his daughter, France, in *Daughters and Sons*. He is a novelist who earns enough to keep his large family, not without stress. We know nothing about him as writer except his popularity, hard work and professional jealousy, but when France writes a novel, some details remind us of her author: it is dramatic enough to be easily adapted for a village play, 'in the family sphere which comprised her experience' (87), 'a string of beads' (92) and with 'differentiated' characters (99). John's character is most vivid in personal relations: with his sister and secre-tary, Hetta, who proves less indispensable to him and the family than she makes out; his second wife, Edith, with whom he has a 'rather wist-ful friendship' (161), and marries for bad reasons; and France, whose novel is good enough to make him dissuade her from publishing but not stop her using a pseudonym and winning a prize – which she gives him anonymously. Less intense, physical and possessive than father–daughter loves in *Elders and Betters* and *The Mighty and Their Fall*, their deep affection is at the heart of the novel.

The fourth imaginary professional writer is Hereward Egerton in *A God and His Gifts,* another best-seller whose popularity compromises his creative powers, and whose character is central to the action. His rival is his son, Merton, keen to please the few and not the many, who loved his father's story-telling when he was young but grows to despise it. He works hard, once almost coming to the point of submitting a book, but we know he will never publish anything. Hereward supports and dominates his large family, including his philistine father, Sir Michael, who feels he could write a novel – 'such a light sort of thing' (17) – if he put his mind to it, and a butler ashamed that his employer is a household word. Happy, moral and silly, Sir Michael repeats the idea which so infuriates novelists, that anyone can write a novel because it needs no training. We see something of Hereward at work: cut off from domestic routine, absorbed and obsessed by his characters, vacant and lost when he finishes a book. As the title suggests, his gifts are godlike in more ways than one: his serial fertile seductions and sympathetic, fatherly affections are Zeus-like. He goes in for exultant outbursts of creative pride which are more egocentric and less humanist than those of Claverhouse. This is how he speaks to his mistress, who says that she knows him and he knows himself: 'I do. I wish I did not. I know the forces within me. I know they may rise up at any time. I don't exhaust them on my work. They are not easily spent' (8). This is how he describes himself to his family, romantically converting confession to boast:

> 'I am a man of great powers, swift passions and a generous heart. You have met them all, benefited by most, suffered from some . . .
>
> . . . I have cheered the homes of thousands. I have served our family home.' (131–2)

The writers in *Pastors and Masters* are creative only in lies: Nicholas Herrick is a would-be plagiarist, who pretends to give up scholarship for fiction, and Richard Bumpus pretends to be writing a new novel instead of his first, which he buried in a friend's grave, but prudently keeping a copy.

There are real writers celebrated in the novels, not used structurally, as Twain and Joyce used Homer, but usually to shed light on their fictitious readers. Shakespeare and Tennyson are often quoted. Dickens is praised and criticised. The Greek and Latin drama the novelist had studied are rarely mentioned, but when they are, the allusion is telling.

Austen was the novelist admired by the only imaginative man in *Pastors and Masters*, and he is followed by Nance in *A House and Its Head*: '"My father is come!" quoted Nance. "He is in the hall at this moment"' (103): we are told and shown it is a quotation but not given the source. There is no obvious similarity between the situation in this household and that at the end of Volume I of *Mansfield Park*, since the younger Edgeworths are only modestly entertaining a few neighbours, not rehearsing a scandalous play in dangerously mixed company, and the unannounced return of Duncan is no occasion for alarm. But the parallel with Sir Thomas Bertram is not entirely inappropriate because this father's arrival also brings unwelcome change – he roughly announces his engagement to a young woman, who will take their mother's place. His browbeating of wife and children make him incomparably worse than autocratic and eventually repentant Sir Thomas, but *Mansfield Park* also contains the tyrannical Mrs Norris. Nance is a rational and caring character and she is made a good Austen reader as a mark of favour, or we can put it the other way round and suggest that only favoured characters are allowed to love Austen.

In *Two Worlds and Their Ways*, another Austen allusion is made by the governess Miss Petticott, who says after the party for the children's friends that the day 'has been nothing but pleasure from beginning to end, as someone said in a book' (303). Unlike Nance, whose quotation marks tell us she knows her source, Miss Petticott does not remember hers but she is quoting accurately, from Mrs Norris picking on Fanny on the way home from Sotherton: 'Well, Fanny, this has been a fine day for you . . . Nothing but pleasure from beginning to end.'[6] The pertinent quotation adds a nuance to character and a post-script to the scene, and it is a cool intertextual touch of the kind Austen likes: 'Alas! If the heroine of one novel be not patronized by the heroine of another, from whom can she expect protection and regard?'[7]

Critics made much of George Eliot's presence in *Dolores*, in particular, echoes of 'Amos Barton' from *Scenes of Clerical Life*, and Dorothea in *Middlemarch*. In a comic tribute, Gertrude Doubleday in *Manservant and Maidservant* is so proud of her resemblance to George Eliot in physiognomy and philosophy that she hangs a portrait on her wall to make sure visitors spot the likeness. In *Daughters and Sons*, there is an allusion to George Eliot's novella, *The Lifted Veil*, not popular or much discussed in Compton-Burnett's day. Dr Chaucer is a brash clergyman, who asks Edith Hallam, 'May I come to what is in my mind?', to which she replies, 'I think you had better not. There is a story about someone who saw into people's minds, and it was impossible for him. And what is the good of not being able to see into them, if you are told about it?' (144). The convoluted reply, lost on her suitor, seems to refer to George Eliot's Latimer, for whom the veil separating minds is tragically lifted, and though Edith has no idea that Chaucer is going to propose, what she says and the way she says it mark their difference and prepare us for her refusal.

There are allusions to Sophocles in *Darkness and Day* (1951), when Bridget mistakenly thinks she has married her father and says 'we have been brave enough ourselves not to put out our eyes. Perhaps people are braver than they used to be' (112), and her mother-in-law says, 'perhaps fashions have changed. It does not seem that Oedipus was thought to have acted oddly under the circumstances. Or to have been thought exacting in requiring his daughter's attendance for the rest of his days' (117). Another allusion to Greek tragedy comes later, when Edmund says his wife has 'lived with a sense of pursuit. She was always looking over her shoulder at the threat behind. And now she has turned and grappled with it, for all our sakes' (113). The joking irony is replaced by the reference to the Furies in Aeschylus' *Oresteia*, an allusion which is loving and grave in tone, and deepens our knowledge of characters and relationship.[8]

The bad readers are usually amusing, though in *Dolores* the satire is laboured, as when Mrs Blackwood gushes, 'Think what an immense difference in the world of thought' if 'Shakespeare, or Browning, or Milton had never been born' (77), says Milton's language is 'so good' and his 'rhythm always so accurate', and he transports her to ancient Greece and Rome (78). This kind of caricature is not subtle, but it is part of the novel's contrast between a shallow culture and the creative experience of real art. *Pastors and Masters* is about a pretentious culture, as well as a bad school: there is a dinner-party where one man boasts of reading all European literature as well as knowing his Greek and Latin; a woman says she reads only history and biography; another will read anything as long as it is not English, 'if not French, Italian or German'; and the science don, William Masson keeps us in touch with integrity by saying he mostly reads Austen and regrets her early death, provoking the Reverend Francis Fletcher to say he 'has very little use for books written by ladies for ladies' (93–4).

The jokes are better and the satire more controlled in *Men and Wives*. Mrs Christy, mother of the promiscuous and delightful Camilla, is almost a caricature, but a comic contrast to the sincerely and destructively intense Harriet Haslam, and like her daughter she is a welcome relief in a dark novel. She makes few appearances but each makes a mark: she 'suspect[ed] that she had a remarkable brain and found that her spontaneous conversation proved it beyond her hopes'. She packs each clause with metaphor, wit and quotation:

'you are a living proof that absence makes the heart grow fond ... I always think that every mind, at whatever point it is situated in the mental scale, is the better for being laid on the whetstone and sharpened to its full keenness.'

She is proud of her reading and her speech: 'You and Camilla find my parlour constricted, but "stone walls do not a prison make" to minds whose innocence takes them for an hermitage. I had almost taken refuge in some oft-quoted lines' (47); 'I fear that lines rise to my mind at every juncture'; 'quotation, description, analysis, anything is grist to my mill'; and 'My English is of the plainest. A few good words, a few expressions sanctified by long usage, welded easily into a cultivated whole!' (48). She boasts of a need and 'instinct' to 'lose myself in the masters of bygone days, especially in those in affinity with myself' (103), but her best stroke is to quote Christina Rossetti's 'There is a Budding Morrow in Midnight' in self-compliment: 'Matthew's thoughtfulness for me makes me really inclined to say, "Winter is the mother-nurse of Spring, lovely for her daughter's sake"' (214). Compton-Burnett can sacrifice good poems for a good laugh.

It is the other way round in *A House and Its Head*, where Dulcia comments on a proposed party, after a bereavement, 'They only feel it will mark their taking up the common round again' (96). She is using the banal misquotation to which John Keble's fine hymn, 'Morning' from *The Christian Year* (1827), has been reduced:

The trivial round, the common task,
Can furnish all we ought to ask;
Room to deny ourselves; a road
To bring us, daily, nearer God.

Dulcia rushes in where everyone fears to tread, but is overtaken by the good woman, Beatrice, better read in religious literature, who smugly caps the misquotation with the actual line – 'The trivial round, the common task' – to have it unrecognised by her cousin, Rosamund, an ex-missionary less well acquainted with the poet, who obtusely objects, 'I don't know why the party should be called trivial' (96). The misquotation, correction and repetition show the trio of do-gooders doing their act, but the allusion draws attention to Keble's poem, and if we remember it or look it up, it reminds us of its quality and modifies the novelist's usual caricature of Christian virtue.

Keble's words are less resonant in *A Family and a Fortune* when Justine, a sympathetic version of the bouncy good woman, quotes the snippet tritely but correctly as 'common task' (189). Justine has already used literary quotation to express her delight in her Uncle Dudley's unexpected and large inheritance, at the expense of Christina Rossetti's 'My heart is like a singing-bird' (124). Like all the family, she takes her uncle's generosity for granted, and the ecstatic lyrical outburst is in character and mildly ironic.

In *A Father and His Fate*, family talk is rich in quotation: Shake-speare's *As You Like It* is quoted by Constance, 'Sweet are the uses of adversity,' as she looks back to the bad time when they thought their mother dead and their father got engaged to a young woman. The sceptical Ursula says they did not find the uses of adversity sweet, Constance piously believes they 'may have led us upward', and Audrey disagrees: 'They did the opposite' ... and 'I feel I have suffered and deserve amends' (148). Later, Audrey observes their aunt is always watching their mother, now restored to the family, and Ursula says, 'I do not wonder ... One sees what someone meant, when he thanked the gods that dead men rise up never' – a line from 'The Garden of Proserpine'. Their hypocritical father, Miles, says he would not thank them, being 'one of the rare people who have had it happen'. Constance identifies the poet: 'It was Swinburne who wrote the words.' Miles is not impressed: 'Well, Swinburne is wrong as far as I am concerned.' And Verena, whom Miles had planned to marry, pointedly demurs, 'It was a wise thing to say.' He disagrees again: 'No, no, it was not. It was written for effect, and to sound wise by being unexpected. I don't say it has no truth.' An unidentified speaker, probably Verena, objects, 'It must either have the whole truth or none,' and Miles, who took her from his son and returned her, says condescendingly and faithlessly, 'I shall have another daughter who bewilders me' (169–70).

Miles is too jealous to admire poets, too sexist to admire women poets. In a smug, grandiose speech about heritage, he inadvertently quotes a line of Christina Rossetti's 'Italia, io ti saluto', a poem about nostalgia, made relevant but quoted out of context: 'I shall live on in my grandchildren, here where I was born, bred, look to die.' When told by the informative Constance that he is 'quoting a poem', he denies it – 'No, I am not. The words came into my head of their own accord. And I never quote other people. I use my own words or none' – and, later, 'I suppose the poet and I said the same thing. We might easily do that, I mean we might by chance. I don't suppose there is much difference between poets and ordinary – and other people.' He is infuriated when Constance says it was a woman: 'A poetess? . . . Well of course I was not quoting her.' Asked if he objects to quoting a woman, he replies, 'I should not quote anyone. And naturally I should not quote a woman. What man would?' Audrey observes, 'A man did.' Miss Gibbon encourages his sexism: 'Would a woman quote a man . . .?' Miles says, 'I suppose so, if she quoted anyone. She would not quote another woman.' Constance tells them the poet is Christina Rossetti and, in 'a manner of meeting success himself', Miles objects, 'Rossetti was a man' but, being told 'Christina was his sister,' concludes, 'Oh, he had a sister? Well, that was different. I suppose it ran in the family. That proves what I said' (205–6).

The wildest and funniest literary allusion comes in *Mother and Son* where Emma and Hester are dominated by the cat called Plautus. The new housekeeper, like the author not a cat-lover, is not able to avoid his company and keep her job. After the cat-loving Emma 'swiftly' interprets her polite 'He is a beautiful cat' (40) – 'So you do not care for cats, dear' – she asks about his name and is told he is called after a not very good Latin playwright because 'He hasn't written any good plays either' (41). The realistic psychological drama in which Plautus stars amazed Ivy's cat-loving friends, who, in real life, had to make sure she did not encounter their cats (or dogs).[9] The joke was on them, and a brilliant piece of zany humour by the expert on jokes.

In *Mother and Son*, a little learning is again the subject of a joke. There is a lunch party where the hostess, Emma Greatheart, is afraid her new housekeeper, Miss Burke, might be thinking of leaving:

'How you frightened me for the moment!'
  'Were you imagining yourself without her?' said Hester.
  'I almost dared to fear that she was imagining it. And a coward soul is mine.'

'That strikes an echo somewhere,' said Rosebery. 'I do not remember who had the coward soul.'

'You should remember who did not have it,' said Miss Burke.

There was a pause. (88)

The allusions to Emily Brontë are in character: Rosebery's vague memory, Emma's neat adaptation and Miss Burke's mild, ironic correction of 'No coward soul', which Rosebery will not understand. Unlike Miles and the clergyman in *Pastors and Masters* who dismisses ladies who write for ladies, Rosebery is not misogynist but just rather dim.

The allusions are often of this kind, mild jokes just right for the character, as when the ironist, Rachel Hardisty, says, as I mentioned in Chapter 6, that she hates 'people whose golden bowls are broken' (153); this is one of the most amusing literary allusions, even better if we know that Compton-Burnett was often asked if James had influenced her.[10] In *The Present and the Past*, poetry is not only upstairs with Megan's mole poem and Blake's 'Infant Joy' but also in the kitchen quartet: Ainger, the butler; Mrs Frost, the cook; and Kate and Madge, the upper and lower housemaids, who are inclined to be socially subversive. After Cassius dies, Madge's irreverent adaptation of Andrew Marvell's 'Horatian Ode on the Death of King Charles the First' is as clever as Emma's Brontë: 'I wish they had something common done or mean, upon that memorable scene.' Obsequious Ainger says, 'The words apply,' Simon, the page, asks who did nothing common or mean, and Mrs Frost says, 'It was only once that it was anyone.' Kate's joke, 'Someone who was to be beheaded . . . It would be hard to be oneself then,' is capped by the cook, 'Anyhow for long', but Ainger concludes loyally, 'It was Charles the First of England . . . Charles, our Royalist king' (117). The many-toned, witty choric commentary seems even more politically nuanced if we remember that the poem even-handedly celebrates Oliver Cromwell and the King.

Sometimes allusion has no connection with individual speaker. In *The Mighty and Their Fall*, Ninian asks his children, 'Are you all at a solemn music? Or has silence a music of its own?' (8). His quotation from Milton's 'At a Solemn Music' has no significance for character but the poetry and Ninian's formal sentences are in keeping with the novel's prevailing style. This rises to rhythmical and imagistic language, biblical echo and short, balanced sentences, as formal and stylised as the poetic passages in *Darkness and Day*, but more reflexive and without psychological and thematic emphasis. For instance, Ninian's brother,

Ransom, returns from exile to proclaim, 'I have come back to have my way. I am the man I was . . . Money comes to the just and unjust. It has come in a measure to me. I have resisted temptation and yielded to it' (106). Their mother, the tyrannical but not unsympathetic Selina, parodies Mark Antony's oration in *Julius Caesar*:

'Agnes and Hengist and Leah, lend me your ears. I come to bury something, not to praise it. The mistake your father made will not live after him. I have come to end it with a word. It is a word you will hear in silence . . . Your father is not going to be married.' (56)

The adopted son, Hugo, declaims a fine meta-textual *précis*: 'There is material for an epic. The fall of Lavinia; the return of Ransom; the uplift of Ninian; the tragedy of Ransom; the escape of Lavinia; the lament of Selina' (115). Her brother, Egbert, tells Lavinia, 'I have seen you as the heroine of a drama' (98), and when Selina dies, Hugo wishes he were Dickens to do justice 'without restraint' to her character as a 'great woman' (171). Here too there is poetry downstairs, the butler, Ainger – a second and more subversive Ainger – concluding with another formal summary:

'Some people are put too high. They fail in their own sphere. The master and Miss Lavinia; the old master and Mr Hugo; and the old mistress in a way. Ah, I have heard, and said to myself, "Ah, how are the mighty fallen!"' (184)

The novel has its own emphatic literary style, and responds to its title. How does the artist represent creative art? How does the artist represent the recipient? What do we read and remember? What do we quote and why? What makes a reader good or bad? Compton-Burnett is like many novelists in drawing portraits of the artist, unusual in representing so many readers. Of course, there are precedents in Cervantes, Austen, Eliot, Hardy and James, but their readers are central and conspicuous. Eliot and Hardy also show reading as part of the novelist's experience, in narration, but Compton-Burnett mediates literature through all her characters. She knew that much of the day for men, women and children – in her time, of more than one class – was passed in reading and talking about books, and she shows this experience in ways which not only contribute to theme, psychology and plot but, like eating, drinking and talking, are a part of culture, language and daily life.

Notes

1. Compton-Burnett disliked music, perhaps because her sisters were musical, perhaps because she found the earlier or contemporary music she would have heard too intensely expressive.
2. Hilary Spurling, *Secrets of a Woman's Heart*, 265–6.
3. Michael Millgate, 'Interview with Miss Compton-Burnett', in *The Art of I. Compton-Burnett*, ed. Burkhart, 37.
4. Margaret Jourdain and Ivy Compton-Burnett, 'A Conversation between I. Compton-Burnett and Margaret Jourdain', in *The Art of I. Compton-Burnett*, ed. Burkhart, 23.
5. See Burkhart's Introduction to the second edition of *Dolores*, 1971.
6. *Mansfield Park*, Volume 1, Chapter 10.
7. *Northanger Abbey*, Chapter 5.
8. See Chapter 10 for a fuller discussion of references to Greek tragedy in *Darkness and Day*.
9. Spurling, *Secrets of a Woman's Heart*, 199.
10. *Men and Wives*, Chapter 6, 72; 88.

Chapter 9

Elders and Betters

Elders and Betters (1944) presents Compton-Burnett's world of country house, family and servants at its most enclosed. There are two related families, the Donnes and the Calderons: one with father, children, middle-aged cousin, housekeeper distantly related to the family, and two servants; the other with parents, children, mother's invalid sister, governess, her niece and almost invisible servants. Benjamin Donne and his adult sons are civil servants; Thomas Calderon is a critic and journalist, who would prefer to be just 'a writer', his wife, Jessica, and sister-in-law, Sukey, having just sufficient private incomes. Death and sex spin the plot. Family relations become more intense after Sukey Donne's death from heart disease and Jessica's from suicide, and the other crucial events are Anna Donne's engagement to her cousin, Terence, Thomas's to Florence Lacy, Florence's re-engagement to Bernard Donne, and Tullia Calderon's subsequent engagement to Bernard. There are three bright children, Reuben Donne, Dora and Julius Calderon. The time of action is set back to the beginning of the century, as we know from family size, unemployment of upper-class women, employment of tutor, governess and servants, and a class gap which is explicitly discussed.

There is a concentration on one character, unusual in these novels, and that character, Anna Donne, is wholly unsympathetic. She performs three deliberated and wicked acts: she burns Sukey's will to gain an inheritance, brainwashes Jessica and drives her to kill herself, and pretends Jessica wanted her to marry Terence. After Jessica's death, Thomas gets engaged to Florence; his daughter Tullia reveals her jealous love for him, and he realises that he wants her more than a second marriage. The sub-plot cannot compete with the main plot in depth and vitality, and ends in a flurry of pairings, but the main psychological action is so absorbing, so original and so disconcerting that this scarcely matters.

This action is kept wholly within the family, with no surrounding community, and no visits or voyages. There is a marked unity of place and time – just a tactfully unspecified time for Thomas to mourn Jessica's death and plan to marry again. Cousin marriage is the norm, and *cousinage* indeed proves a *dangereux voisinage*, but filial intimacy is hazardous too: Thomas tells Tullia she is irreplaceable and they are seen locked in each other's arms. Compton-Burnett is good at dramatising sensuous and passionate relationships without coyness, showing strong impulsive touch or embrace without necessarily suggesting sexual relations. This is not one of the novels where incest is involved, like *Brothers and Sisters* and *A House and Its Head*, but the recycling of relationships, within a small, closed circle where sickness, death and ill-wishing prevail, helps to create a sinister atmosphere – a family loucheness. Animosity is a feature of these intimate relations: no one does family rudeness better than Compton-Burnett, and it ranges from Anna's accusation that Jessica darkens her family's life to Anna's announcement of her engagement, where her family's amazement adds a comic touch.

The recurring dialogue of the servants, Ethel and Cook, is not a result of what the novelist sometimes saw as necessary 'interpolation'[1] but a chorus with protective Ethel and hypochondriac Cook as critical presences. Their first interchange includes a laconic comparison of benevolent Miss Jennings (Jenney) and nagging Anna: 'We can't estimate the privilege of living with her'; 'Such an example, and before our eyes'; 'You would think Miss Anna would be influenced by her'; '"A leopard can't change his spots"' (24). Such commentary runs ironically through the book. In Greek drama, the chorus of ordinary citizens sometimes overlaps with the functional messenger, and in *Elders and Betters* an internet of servants and tradesmen transmits news at top speed, here just between the two houses which are separated by a walking distance. This is social media delivering the narrative of family life, in self-styled creative gossip.

The Calderon children, Julius and Dora, also form a chorus, pathetic, funny and poetically eloquent, as it re-invents religious ritual in play, mimicking adult culture but childlike in bonding, squabbling, fighting, giggling, over-loved and neglected, desperate for security and space. The children are now and then patronised by the elders who are not their betters, but never by their author. Their make-believe and critique are delightful and their knowing innocence a good choric qualification. The children pray, narrate, comment and judge from the verge of action and responsibility:

'For our mother's place is filled, and the hand of the step-mother will be over us. Let it not be a harsh sway, O god . . . Our brother and sister go into the homes of the stranger, and our governess, thy handmaid, does not see us with a mother's eyes. But put kindness for us into her heart . . .' (291)

Sometimes, as on this occasion, the 'great and good and powerful god, Chung' (291), whom they have created, answers their wonderfully articulate prayers.

Idiolect and action bring out moral quality. The Donnes arrive at their new house, chosen by Anna and her father and which no one else in the family has seen. As they criticise or praise it, they reveal their complacency, insensitivity, humour, humourlessness, altruism and egoism. The bumpy domestic routine on moving-day introduces character and moral type, and prepares sensational developments, but it is the stuff of everyday life – new rooms, lost luggage which is not really lost, taxi fare and tips, family visits and family chat about children growing taller, grown-ups ageing, looks, money, illness – Sukey, Jessica, Reuben and Cook are variously afflicted – lessons, games and meals. One by one, the characters are introduced and moved on in the diurnal flow till the crucial actions begin. As usual, narrative and description give way to conversation, though the key actions of Anna take place in solitude and secrecy, witnessed only by the readers, brought disturbingly close to a character with whom they can neither identify nor sympathise.

Compton-Burnett insisted that plot was essential, seeing it as structure or 'bones'.[2] From beginning to end, the painful action is combined with comedy, in conversation and action, like the children's private religious ritual, and striking scenes like the luncheon party – discussed in Chapter 6 – where the eating and drinking are suspended by the fear of being thirteen at table. The action has an ending in which everyone seems to relax contentedly, apart from Jessica, the one character capable of great love, whose lack of self-esteem exposes her to Anna's power.

Despite the superficially happy ending, *Elders and Betters* is the most uncomfortable of the novels because of Anna, guilty of lies, theft, deception and – morally, if not legally – of murder. She gets away scot-free, rich, happy and with the man she wants, and we are forced to share her guilty secret, which is never made public. The linguistic self-consciousness of these novels usually creates a distance between reader and character but here it is qualified by unusual intimacy and knowledge. We are made to feel not for, but with, the entirely unsympathetic character, who, from the start, occupies centre-stage. She could be thought of as usurping the place of a heroine if it were not for the fact that these novels – perhaps with the exception of *Darkness and Day* – do not have heroines.

To start with an action no one sees but the reader: Sukey Donne, rich, unmarried and demanding, dies of heart disease while Anna, her niece and brand-new family favourite, has been reading to her, and Anna purloins Sukey's impulsively made new will, which Sukey has asked her to destroy. Instead, Anna burns the old will in favour of sister Jessica, with whom Sukey often quarrels but whom she loves and who has loved and cared for her:

> Anna read aloud . . . Sukey listened with her eyes closed, and gave no sign of the moment when she slept. Anna read until the sleep was sound, and then closed the book and rose to go, taking the scroll from the table. It seemed as if Sukey knew what she did, for her face settled into youth and calm. Anna looked at her and looked again; stood as if she hardly knew where she was; approached her and touched her hand and her face; made a movement to the desk, and drew back and glanced round the room, as if to make sure she was alone. (131)

The topos of supposition in those three 'as ifs' insists that we see only Anna's physical movements and only infer her state of mind. We read her recognition of death, her first impulse to carry out her aunt's instruction – 'made a movement to the desk' – her realisation that death has changed everything, and finally her temptation to take the old will out of the desk. Similarly observed from the outside, Anna leaves, carrying the second will which she was told to destroy, 'showing neither furtiveness nor haste', and we read that she 'seemed prepared' (131).

We observe her otherwise unobserved journey home, and then observe her burning the will Sukey told her to preserve: 'She still maintained her natural air; she might have been acting to herself' (132). After these observations, there follows an exceptional penetration of her mind by the narrator: 'Anna remembered that walls have ears and eyes' (132). This seems to be permitted because the author knows the reader will have inferred the guilty act. The flexibility of free indirect style allows a move from the 'walls have ears', which sounds like Anna's idiolect, to the less banal 'ears and eyes'.

Until she burns the will in her own drawing-room, Anna is on the alert, 'acting to herself', prepared to meet someone and explain, and the only observer, the reader, breathes, fears, and prepares with her as she glances 'about in readiness to exchange a greeting', with a 'word ready for anyone who asked for it' (131–2). The matter-of-fact, precise description of her nervy but cunning behaviour is highly expressive, signifying character and pacing the reader. Anna meets no one on the road, sees no one in the house, and the way is cleared for her future acting, lying, and preservation of the secret. We are with her every step of the way and beat of the heart, in her silence and her solitude and her nervousness and her criminal cunning, and we feel the pressure of that closeness.

Anna is unusual amongst Compton-Burnett characters not only in her successful secret wrong-doing but in her unrelieved immorality, which is totally revealed to the reader. Sybil in *A House and Its Head* is a nasty, unscrupulous, murdering creature, motivated solely by cupidity, and though we do not know her child victim, who is kept off-stage, as we know Jessica, he is a helpless infant and the murder sneakingly carried out by blackmail and commission. But Sybil is not constantly at the centre of the narrative, like Anna, and more importantly, she is subjected to shaming exposure (though not to everyone). Matthew in *Men and Wives* is a more sympathetic murderer, and though Compton-Burnett ironically allows his possessive mother to have her way after death, the murder is a complex act of love which shakes the murderer to his core. Horace Lamb in *Manservant and Maidservant* is a mean, cruel father and husband who is exposed and punished, and undergoes a kind of conversion and reform. In *Two Worlds and Their Ways*, the parents and their children lie, cheat and steal but they are sympathetic characters and their wrong-doing is justified, forgiven and consoled. Closest to Anna is Josephine in *More Women than Men*, who is also not technically a murderer, and who also gets away with lies, hypocrisy, deception and husband-stealing; she is never punished for what she has done, and is rewarded with a happy ending, but she is exposed, though the witness of her guilt can love her. But there is a witness, and the reader is not burdened with knowledge and proximity.

Almost every character in every novel is likely to lie, steal, plagiarise, deceive, cheat, betray and seduce, without being punished or blamed, or morally categorised. The novels show and say that we are all egocentric and afraid to die, and *Elders and Betters* cleverly demonstrates this in the superstitious luncheon party. But after Anna destroys Jessica, for whom deceit is so appalling that other vices are virtues in comparison, we watch her getting away with it, to subvert all traditions of poetic justice. Heartless Anna is the heart of this novel, looming large from the beginning, charmless, bossy, un-self-critical, clumsy, rude, rough, hard, deceitful, destructive and callous – and the reader stays close to her. Other writers seem sentimental and untruthful in comparison with Compton-Burnett, not a writer who wants to stimulate emotion, but an analyst of emotion, and the reading experience is not wholly a pleasure. *Elders and Betters* shows this more plainly than any of the other novels.

The reading is not exactly a pleasure but it is an education. As I have said, Compton-Burnett shows and analyses many forms of narrative, and in this novel she scrutinises the psychology of lying. Anna is not a brilliant liar, no Machiavellian planner like Richard of Gloucester, Iago or Edmund, no improviser like Odysseus or Huckleberry Finn, only a fairly lucky and very determined opportunist. The nature of her lying is dramatised and demonstrated in conversation scenes in which the reader is made to concentrate on her words. After one or two lying scenes – really rehearsals – in which she simply asserts that her aunt Sukey died feeling resentful and neglected, we watch her in more elaborate episodes where she stumbles in story-telling as she does in physical movement. Because she is not a good improviser, people pick up clues from her mistakes: after she lies about her aunt burning papers in her room, her brother Reuben mentions a smell of burning in their house (where she has burnt the will in favour of Jessica), and she gets away with her explanation in spite of blundering into another lie, which, in its turn, involves two or three more. Like more exalted forms of art, lies are self-generative:

> 'There was a live coal on this rug ... It spurted out of the fire. It was a good thing I was there to stop it smouldering. I had just come back from Aunt Sukey and could have dispensed with being startled at that moment.'
>
> 'But you didn't know that she was dead,' said Reuben.
>
> 'No, but I knew that she was ill and exhausted. It gave me a sort of nervous feeling to be with her. It seems that I ought to have guessed more than I did.' (163)

But Reuben is not a detective and she gets away with the new lies.

Lie spawns lie again in a claustrophobic scene where the two women, Anna and Jessica, confront each other in Sukey's room, where Jessica has forced Anna to re-enact the death scene. Anna invents a story about Sukey promising her a photograph, and Jessica spots something wrong: 'She never had her photograph taken' (175). Anna has to wriggle out of her false and faulty narrative, and she goes more slowly, playing for time, taking more care, using her intelligence and finally coming up with a distracting self-deprecation and hesitation:

> 'Or have I got it twisted in some way? That would be rather in my character. I asked her if she would have her portrait painted. And she said she would give me a photograph of it, if she ever did. I think that was it.' (175)

This is a better lie, and it works, but then, pushed to describe Sukey's last scene in more detail, she pushes her luck, with an invented detail about Sukey folding her hands which is rejected by Jessica, playing the part of interrogator: 'Sukey never folded her hands' (197). Anna has to keep going, so fumbles her way by trial and error into a more acceptable invention, eventually warming to her work and playing for time as she imagines another alternative, then another plausible self-praising excuse for getting something wrong, this time a wish to spare Jessica the detail.

> 'Oh, well, idle in her lap. No, I don't think she did fold them. Actually they were working on her lap, but there did not seem to be any need to press that home. They were closing and unclosing, if you must have the scene as it was. You make it quite impossible to save you anything.' (197)

And this success encourages her to push aggression even further, doing very well with an accusation of neglect: 'And how can you say positively what she did? You did not watch her quite so faithfully, or that was not her impression' (197).

The revisionary lie works: '"I can imagine her hands working," Jessica said, once again speaking to herself' (197). The dangerous corners are rounded successfully, Anna helped by the innocence of this interlocutor, as she was by Reuben when she told her first big lie. One lie is consolidated by others, as she moves from self-defence to begin the process of demoralising and destroying her vulnerable aunt. And it is all done by conversation, designed to be followed word by word, stop by stop, by the slow and careful reader.

Anna's lack of imagination makes it necessary for her to build on a solid groundwork of fact, and her lack of invention and high intelligence encounter Jessica's absolute truthfulness, offering an opportunity for her own easy false construction: her best story, which kills Jessica, is one of those lies which is a part-truth. This truth is Jessica's dark, brooding self-doubt, which opens her dangerously – in the end, fatally – to Anna's kind of lying: in this case, to accuse is to excuse herself most successfully.

By her own imaginative elimination of psychological impossibilities, Jessica does come momentarily to suspect Anna, innocently and spontaneously revealing her suspicion, but innocently spurring her to more aggression and giving her a dangerous opening:

> 'Anna,' said Jessica, in a tone that held no sudden difference, but seemed to come from gathering purpose, 'if you ever wanted to tell me anything, you would not be afraid? . . . You would not hesitate?' There was a just perceptible pause. (198)

Even suspicion is limited; the truthful and loving Jessica can just about imagine temptation and susceptibility, but not a character as thoroughly and uncompromisingly devious as Anna's, so she plays into her hands. The reader can perceive the reason for that 'just perceptible pause' provided by the rare narrative commentary, here once again restricted to an account of behaviour, drawing the reader's attention to it, as Anna recovers herself and can almost joke about her hesitation, turning uncertainty into advantage, and also able to indulge in the luxury of using a truth, with the first words, 'Indeed I should':

> 'Indeed I should,' said Anna, almost with a laugh. 'You are the last person I would face in such a situation . . . You would make anyone feel a criminal, indeed might make anyone be one. I begin to feel my mind reflecting your own. It must be ghastly to have such seething depths within one.'
> Jessica looked into her niece's face.
> 'I wonder if other people see me like that.' (198)

We follow four pages of devastating dialogue in which Anna generates her imagined and invented story about Jessica's destructive imagination, fascinatingly created by her own destructiveness and imagining a criminal conscience which she herself does not possess. She is telling another of those half-truths, on this occasion deadly.

This is a striking example of the relationship of form and feeling. The reader feels discomfort, as the dialogic form insists. Along with the lack of moral consequence, the replacement by high reward of the usual punishment we expect in fiction, go the formal confinement and isolation of the reader, the only one to share the author's authority. Methodically and impulsively, Anna generates the story which destroys Jessica's self-belief, identity and her life, and there is no observation or judgement made by the author. Not for the reader of this dialogic novel the reassuring, wise voice setting the moral context, comic and ironic like Thackeray's commentary on Becky Sharp in *Vanity Fair*, or grave and compassionate like George Eliot's analysis of Arthur in *Adam Bede* or Tito in *Romola*. The narrator in Compton-Burnett stays outside the action.

Anna's destructive pressure on Jessica is frighteningly effective because it is all performed by words, shown by this word-expert to break bones as effectively as sticks and stones. The aggression is the more hideous because the novelist is imagining imagination at work, and in words. It is formed like an artist's imagination, a self-generated writing-in-speaking, starting with spontaneous, instinctive self-defence, growing self-conscious and thoughtful, culminating in effectively generalising sensuous imagery, allusion and paradox, growing in eloquence – 'You are like some dark angel, honestly and unselfishly serving the cause of evil' (203) – luxuriously daring truths, as when she is asked to be precise – 'It is all vague and nameless to me' and 'So, if you like, say I have imagined it' (203). In the comic creation of a less dangerous liar, the nursery-maid, Bertha Mullet, in *Parents and Children*, whom I have quoted, the author slyly points out the liar's use of truth, but here she leaves it to the reader to make it out and take it in.

Sometimes in this novel the feelings are explained and analysed by the narrator but in Anna's lying the reader almost always has to infer feelings which are not described or narrated. Tone is occasionally indicated, as in the first chapter, when Anna, Claribel and Jenney arrive at the new house: 'rather rough tones', 'a tone of speaking to a child' (6) and 'a tone of appreciation' (7) are psychological clues. But in that crucial dialogue between Anna and Jessica, the behavioural directions are ironies suggesting that tone is only tone-deep, reinforcing our recognition of the difference between surface and depth, statement and truth, as we infer Jessica's honest doubting and her growing susceptibility to the false narrative (very like Othello's doubting and susceptibility) and as we detect Anna's falsity and plausibility (very like Iago's falsity and plausibility). The novelist marks the space between what we have inferred and what we have observed: '"Anna," said Jessica, in a tone that held no sudden difference, but seemed to come from gathering purpose' (198); 'Jessica looked at Anna almost in wonderment, seeming to return from the world of her own thoughts' (200); '"We will leave the matter of the wills," said Jessica, as if her thoughts had been elsewhere' (202); '"A cloud would be lifted from the household, if I were gone," said Jessica, using a tone between statement and question' (200); 'Anna rested her eyes in a new wonderment on her aunt' (203). Repeatedly and in different ways, the topos of supposition scrupulously reminds us that we are inferring Jessica's responses, and of course the novelist is confining such rhetoric to Jessica, since we already know Anna's insincerity, having observed her actions.

Anna's third and concluding lie is to lazy, charming, clever Terence, the cousin she falls in love with and finds she can buy. Once more, luck plays into her clumsy hands as she does her wooing in a drama as fascinatingly improbable as Richard of Gloucester's wooing of Lady Anne over the corpse of her father-in-law. Anna badly needs an opening, and immediately after Jessica's suicide, she gets it and seizes it: Terence says his father has told him that since their income will be reduced he must earn his living, and as he half-jokes about being born indolent, he mentions his mother seriously enough:

'But cannot you really do something more for yourself?'
    'A breadwinner is born, not made. My mother quite understood it.'
    'Then that is what she meant by what she said to me,' said Anna, as if to herself. (234)

Terence's levity, his seriousness about his dead mother, and her own slack style of cliché stand the liar in good stead:

'Did she ask you to adopt me?'
    Anna glanced at him for a moment.
    'You are pretty warm,' she said . . .
    'In what way were you to do it?'
    'Oh, in the way that a woman can adopt a man,' said Anna, in a light, incidental tone.
    'I am touched that my mother was matchmaking for me in her last hours.' (235)

The last line shows Terence's individual touch of serious irony but Anna takes him in because her lie is too big and outrageous to be detected, though he is too sharp not to wonder why Jessica should be so 'kind' as to want Anna for a daughter-in-law, though apparently, as Anna has told him, 'not kind' to her (235). But Anna's improved proficiency in lying shows itself in quick recovery: 'Oh, I don't think I was in her thoughts. I was just the instrument to save you from poverty, or whatever she feared for you' (235), a reply which not only is plausible but also carefully reminds him of his need and her money. He says lightly that it was his father's duty to care for him, then unfairly remarks, still resentful of the advice to work, 'he is like an animal, and takes no thought for me, now I am mature' (235). Anna tells another lie about Jessica's opinion of Florence, cleverly tucked into a generalised reference to 'those who incurred her other words . . . Florence and your father and all of them' (235). He asks, 'Why, what did she say . . . ?' and sharply objects to the less plausible fiction that Jessica thought Florence an unsuitable wife for Terence, 'for material and other reasons', as not 'in the tone of my mother's speech' (235). Anna again uses the luxury of using the truth in a lie, and comes back with her successful, insincere self-deprecation, 'Oh no, it is mine . . . I am not quoting your mother . . . should not dream of it' (235).

Later on, she 'clears the way' for Terence and Florence, 'as if by a carefully unconsidered movement' (244), sitting at a distance with 'her eyes on the pair' (245), joining a coded conversation about love and marriage to address Terence pointedly – 'And you don't take very kindly to labour, do you?' (245) – complacently relishing the rivalry of Florence's charm, confident of the man's weakness and her own economic allure. Bright, indolent Terence will allow himself to be 'adopted' in the way 'a woman can adopt a man' by the charmless, wicked woman who has driven his mother to death. By the end of the three-cornered conversation, it is all up with love. In the next chapter, Anna announces her engagement to her astounded family.

The novelist presents us with a course of moral action which we must follow carefully, with little authorial mediation, in a world in which Anna gets money, man and marriage. Burkhart argues that Anna's bluntness helps to make her sympathetic[3]; however, her plain speaking seems to me in no way an alleviation but, like Iago's 'honesty', a cover and medium for her two-faced lies and plots. It is an assumed and much-paraded candour and modesty which deceive more intelligent people: 'I expect I am still the blundering innocent I always was,' she boasts (288). Here the ironic and complex word 'innocent' raises the dangerous subject of crime and Miss Lacy, the precise governess, spots the cliché and asks why the innocent can be said to blunder when it is criminals who are famous for mistakes. The wit and paradox of sophisticated Terence sparkle in an innocent response:

'We are very unfair to criminals,' said Terence. 'They only make one blunder out of so many. They ought nearly always to have the credit of the crime. What right have we to be so exacting, when we are only criminals at heart?'

'What kind of things do we hide within us?' said Anna, in an idle tone.

'Bad things, but not that the world calls wrong.'

'Hasty judgements, self-satisfaction,' said Miss Lacy. 'Too little understanding.'

'Those are not bad,' said Terence. 'They are the stuff of life itself. Which no doubt means that they are very bad indeed.'

'You are being clever,' said Anna. (288)

And he is, at his most Wildean. But as we read his glib paradox and abstract wisdom, we observe with Anna the limits of clever talk. Early in the novel, the unsophisticated Jenney says the flashing dialogue 'is all about nothing' (38), and here its flightiness is apparent. These clever, innocent speakers scrutinise and discuss language wittily but too abstractly, knowing much less than the guilty, self-styled, blundering innocent – and the reader, so the conversation teems with dramatic irony. Anna is far less clever and original in speech than either but she is cunning enough to get Terence by criminal deceits he and Miss Lacy do not begin to imagine, and she points the innocence of their idle and amusing analysis, during which her own silence and speech are not as 'idle' as her tone suggests in that important narrative direction (288).

Burkhart also thinks it important that Anna's dominance dwindles towards the end of the novel, and it does, but surely because it has succeeded, and winner takes all. The loves of Thomas, Florence, Tullia, Bernard and Esmond move into the foreground and help to wind things up, but they are simple and shallow, characters barely developed, compared with Anna, and her lies will never stop. Florence rapidly exchanges daughter-loving and unimaginative Thomas – whom, we infer, she preferred to lazy, self-serving Terence – for Esmond, who has a safe job in the Civil Service and is the next to offer. The cynical spinsters, observers and outsiders, Claribel and Miss Lacy, prefer celibacy because the grapes of the marriage feast are sour – and they really are. But nothing sweeter is on offer, in this novel. Jenney is sweet but sentimental, undiscriminating, easily satisfied and too self-effacing. She is like other good characters in the novels, who ask too little for themselves and make excellent carers. We may prefer self-effacement to Anna's self-aggrandisement, but we are not given the choice. It seems right that we are left with the children taking comfort, surviving in the religion they have invented. It is only in their company that we are free from Anna's, though we are reminded of her as they remember their dead mother. It is a bleak world, in spite of the wit, the jokes and the fools, but only the reader knows how bleak. The bleakness may be in part inadvertent because the most interesting characters, Anna, Jessica and Sukey, inhabit the main plot, and the sub-plot cannot compare in interest, but this only means that the novelist became engrossed with one story, and one form of feeling, at the expense of another, and the subtleties ran away with her for good reason. It is perhaps no accident that the novel was written in the middle of the war, and took a year longer than her books usually did. If it is a one-sided work, the defect is the defect of an original if chilling achievement.[4]

Compton-Burnett's bleak world has something in common with Thomas Hardy's, as he imagines the tragic imagination, but it is fundamentally unlike his, which is marked by tragically angry and compassionate hankering after the lost concept of Providence, with admiration and pity for thwarted humanity. Compton-Burnett's fiction is neither angry nor compassionate, tragic nor meliorist, but austere and stoical, in a world without God and without any intellectually compromising nostalgia for God. It is also unlike Hardy's novels – and those of the earlier great Victorians – because the readers are made to see the point for themselves, without narrative guidance. We are also left to some extent without sympathetic interiorisation. Hardy offers us access to the inner lives of Marty South, Tess and Jude, soliciting sympathy or empathy as they lose and die, but Compton-Burnett places us outside the consciousness of characters, who only reveal their inner lives in conversation, so partially or imperfectly. We are denied the pleasures of consoling or exalting identification and understanding in this novel, which is so uncomfortably dominated by one character.

To repeat, the austere reliance on dialogue, only superficially interrupted by narrative comment, makes the reading process one of constant scrutiny and inference, which is usually intellectually exhilarating but in this novel is also emotionally and morally disturbing. We are the secret sharers of Anna's lies and secrets, shocked and oppressed in those dialogues with Jessica, as we read and realise the mismatch of a terribly unscrupulous lying with a terribly susceptible listening. The dialogue of teller and listener is a combat and in the end a murder by language, stranger and more shocking, as we are compelled to follow it closely, word by word, than the off-stage murder of the child Richard in *A House and Its Head* or the lovingly staged, inevitable matricide in *Men and Wives*. The dialogue creates a loneliness for the reader, an enforced self-reliance, along with the total absence of fictional consolations, like those of George Eliot's. The other killers in Compton-Burnett,

Sybil Edgeworth, Matthew Haslam and Josephine Napier, are absorbed back into a community which is, to some extent, made aware of their crimes, but what is shockingly different in this novel is the permanent secrecy and silence. The violence and cruelty and lying end up with us, and involve us, not romantically or sublimely or cathartically or pornographically, but coldly. We are left not simply with the absence of commentary and conclusion, the unideal truth – now as then – of unpunished, unstoppable destruction for gain, but also with the contrast between the flattering and comforting lies literature so often tells, and that we lap up. Compton-Burnett is so different from most other writers that she invites us to reflect on the difference. Thackeray intended *Vanity Fair* to make people uncomfortable, and though Compton-Burnett never said so, that is what she does in this novel.

We continue to read Anna's duplicity, success and total lack of remorse in the secret life running on beneath the full, frank and public drama. Her secret is our secret. The text has become sub-text but is the more ironically pronounced – if only these happy-enders knew! – because so much else is made public, because it may be made public, in the almost ceaseless flow of conversation. We read between the lines, alone and helpless.

Greek tragedy suggests itself in the unities, the choruses, the deaths in the enclosed family, and the chain of fatality but what makes Compton-Burnett's novels, especially this one, unlike Greek tragedy is the privacy and secrecy of moral cause and effect. In Greek and Elizabethan tragedy, and indeed in the tragic fiction of certain Victorian novels, there is no moral act which does not bring about a public exposure and a public punishment. Edmund in *King Lear* gets poetic and public justice when his brother, Edgar, kills him in formal combat, and though, for much of the play, his wickedness, like Anna's, is a secret between him and the audience, with consequent dramatic tension and irony, with his defeat and deathbed confession come revelation and recognition. But Compton-Burnett flouts the convention of anagnorisis, and the release, relief and public redress that come with it, and though her guilty people are usually exposed within the family or occasionally in the larger neighbourhood, they are never exposed and punished by the judicial system and, sooner or later, are forgiven and restored to the family and community. In *A House and Its Head*, for instance, Sybil Edgeworth commissions a hideous infanticide, which is investigated and discovered by a neighbour, but kept private, and though she is humiliated by partial exposure, she ends rich, forgiven, satisfied and restored to family and community. *Men and Wives* shows the agonised matricide by Matthew Haslam, but though he loses his lover, he survives and takes up the career he had tried to avoid, which his murdered mother had wanted for him. But in *Elders and Betters*, there is nothing approaching poetic justice, and Anna's wickedness is never discovered, never punished, never regretted. She succeeds, and survives, with no distress whatsoever. Anna is too bad for Aristotle's idea of a tragic hero, and the good are destroyed while the wicked prosper. There is no social consequence, even within the family, and no recognition of the causality, except by villain, author and reader. The novel is an example of what Ortega y Gasset saw as the essential dehumanisation of all art and is prominent in modernism, resisting readers' desire to be so moved by fiction that they participate 'as though it were happening in real life'.[5]

Notes

1. Cicely Grieg wrote, 'Ivy told me "If the book is not long enough I must write some more"' and 'Interpolations . . . is Ivy's word': *Ivy Compton-Burnett*, 25–6.
2. Margaret Jourdain and Ivy Compton-Burnett, 'A Conversation between I. Compton-Burnett and Margaret Jourdain', in *The Art of I. Compton-Burnett*, ed. Burkhart, 26.
3. Charles Burkhart, *I. Compton-Burnett*, 114.
4. Ivy and Margaret spent a lot of time in the country to escape the bombs, occasionally returning to London.
5. José Ortega y Gasset, *The Dehumanization of Art*, 8.

Chapter 10

Darkness and Day

This novel is unusual in structure, with shifts of central character as in *Little Dorrit, Middlemarch* or *War and Peace*, but all joined in one story, and also with concentrated and unified imagery like that of *The Golden Bowl* or *To the Lighthouse*. It is the kind of sprawling form Henry James called 'a large baggy monster',[1] but with its parts paralleled, contrasted, responsive to the symbolic title, very subtly and causally inter-related. Compton-Burnett denied that James influenced her,[2] and thought Virginia Woolf's novels lacked 'bone' and 'character drawing',[3] but I think it is likely that she was unconsciously or consciously influenced by their work. Because it is a novel of character, with a developed moral complexity and concentration, with no action or aspect which is not an important part of the whole, its shifting emphasis works: there is a unity of image and the slow gradual development of one plot even while characters shift from major to minor position and back again. It is a more unified and balanced novel than *Elders and Betters*, where the powerful story of Anna, Sukey and Jessica overshadows the other parts.

In *Darkness and Day* (1951) there are four character centres: one is Sir Ransom Chase; another is Mildred Hallam, the Chase housekeeper–companion and short-serving governess of Rose and Viola; another is the married couple, Bridget and Edmund Lovat, parents of Rose and Viola; and last but certainly not least is the cook, Mrs Spruce. The structure of the novel is Victorian rather than post-Jamesian, as the novelist was certainly aware, because there is an ironic reference to Dickensian form when Rose is asked about *The Old Curiosity Shop*, which she agrees is 'lachrymose', and, when asked if she 'misses things out', says she does, 'to keep to the same people', not liking 'to change to different ones' – one of the many moves to meta-narrative (105). We cannot skip anything in this novel; the characters are not contrasts and parallels in different stories but causally linked in one story, action moving fluently from one to another without marked breaks, but with a shift of centre.

The characters turn out to be closely connected: Sir Ransom is Bridget Lovat's father by Mrs Spruce; Edmund Lovat is Mildred's father by an unknown woman; and so Mildred is Rose and Viola's half-sister. The stories are all linked by the same set of family skeletons, who take their time, and different times, to come out of the cupboard. The children are fond of Sir Ransom, whom they do not know is their grandfather but whose clear-cut features and 'rapid' or 'sudden' dark eyes are clues; they love and are loved by their parents but neglected because of the obsession with their supposed incest; they give Mildred, the governess they do not know is their sister, a hard time, but she discovers her – and their – father Edmund, accepts his provision for her and gives up the teaching and housekeeping. The children have some happy times with Mrs Spruce, whom they do not know is their grandmother. Like the four stories of *Middlemarch*, where characters also shift from centre to periphery and back again, the actions are linked by social, psychological and moral connections. Unlike the stories of *Middlemarch*, however, the stories as well as the characters of *Darkness and Day* are closely connected – it is really all one story.

Mrs Spruce, the cook, is a subdued character who is more of a heroine than anyone else in Compton-Burnett's novels. She is simple and relatively static; if she emerges as the subject of a *Bildungsroman*, it is in an oblique and implicit way. An important and exceptional feature of the novel is its leisurely development within a short time, but what develops is not so much the character as our acquaintance with her. Her past and present are slowly unfolded; not until the end of the last chapter do we understand her nature and quality, and the novel concludes with her solid presence. We never get to know every detail of her history, as we do with Clarissa and Maggie, but we come to appreciate her, as a grown-up woman who accepts her life.

Anna in *Elders and Betters* and Mrs Spruce are moral and psychological opposites, Anna selfish, life-negating and deceitful, Mrs Spruce benign, life-affirming and truthful. They are both placed in an unusual and demanding relation with the readers. Like Anna's destructiveness, Mrs Spruce's integrity is a secret revealed only to us; something of it is understood by her employer, Selina, but only the reader enters her private space, and our access is limited. We are given full access to Anna's secret life, but Mrs Spruce's thoughts and feelings are conveyed in absence, understatement and silence. If we knew less about Anna, she would be less horrifying, and her novelist wants us to be horrified. If we knew everything about Mrs Spruce, she would seem less solitary and self-contained. The author's reticence about her matches her own.

We never know her first name; she is unmarried, the 'Mrs' honorific. Her story is not explicitly political, but it is the story of a cook, a working-class woman, and its feminist implications are inseparable from its critique of class distinction. She is chillingly described by Gaunt Lovat, as he looks at her photograph, as not having 'an educated face' (226). She is thoughtful and perceptive, and her vocabulary is good, though not conspicuous in a kitchen where fellow-servants are more grandly polysyllabic: she uses 'intangible' (64), 'attributes' (66), 'incurred' and 'eluded' (69), 'divergence' (73), 'operated' (73), 'superseded' (75) and 'emulate' (98) – the last speedily emulated by Bartle, the house-boy (99). She does not know the origins of common quotations, as some Compton-Burnett servants do; she uses one or two slightly awkward expressions, such as, 'I was distracted by our intercourse' (101), and 'Mr Ambrose was figurative' (72); and because her punctuation is rudimentary and she cannot manage subordinate clauses, there are sentences without finite verbs in her last letter to her old lover. She feels a deep, unpossessive love for her illegitimate daughter, Bridget, and her granddaughters, Rose and Viola, and keeps the secret of her relationship to them; her story-telling, briefly paraphrased, is loving, like Regan's bird-story in *Parents and Children*. For her former lover, she has had and still has unspecified feelings which are probably erotic and certainly long-lasting, loyal, undemanding and unregretted; it is crucial that, without them, we would think less of him. She is the only important character in the novel whom we may unequivocally admire, so quietly presented that she is scarcely mentioned by critics.

As we have seen, gossip does not have to be falsely fabricated, and in the last two chapters of *Darkness and Day* there is a series of scenes in which rumours and disclosures mingle untruths with truth. At the end of Chapter 6, the little housemaid, Tabitha, tells the others she has seen Edmund Lovat and Mildred Hallam in each other's arms, and there is general speculation: Ambrose, the butler, wonders, 'some kind of jest?' and Bartle thinks the worst, 'failure in morals' (185); Mrs Spruce asks if the children were there and how Tabitha came to see the embrace, then ponders, 'They can hardly have met since the return . . . and before it they were strangers' (186); Alice, the upper maid, proposes a 'Renunciation' worthy of respect, but later suggests 'The moment's impulsiveness' and laments the result, while Tabitha thinks 'it was something we shall never know' (186–7), though they very soon do. Jennet, the maid-cum-butler in the Chace household, arrives and formally announces, 'I have a disclosure,' which turns out to be the news that the embracing couple are father and daughter (190). Mrs Spruce is as tolerant as she dares, warning Bartle he may find 'temptations are rife, as the years go on. And we do not all withstand,' shocking him – 'You talk as if yielding was the natural thing' – and disturbing Ambrose, though he softens his warning that 'Perhaps a stricter line would be in place' with a concession: 'You are led on by largeness of outlook. And that is beyond some,' true in ways he cannot know (192–3).

One of the significant gaps is the response of the kitchen chorus to Sir Ransom's death. It is announced to his best friend, Gaunt, by Mildred in complacent and sentimental mood – 'I have only one thing to say. All is well' and 'He is where he will always be himself, where he will never suffer again' – to be strongly resisted by rational, truth-telling Gaunt – 'So he is dead . . . And you know he did not suffer' (215). Grant meets Mildred's pious 'Well, whatever his mistakes were, he knows now' with 'He knew he would know nothing' (216).

In a fine ellipsis, Mrs Spruce's response to his death is conveyed to the reader indirectly, as it is formally conveyed to Selina though Ambrose: 'Mrs Spruce feels with you, ma'am, and wished me to speak to the effect. Sir Ransom has always been a figure in her eyes.' Selina answers significantly, hinting to the perceptive reader that she has inferred or guessed part of the cook's story, 'I am sure she does. Will you give her our sympathy?' (230).

Sir Ransom's will is discussed by the servants with Fanshawe, the nurse, pleased by the reversionary bequest of the estate to her charges. Alice is speculative – 'I wonder what actuated Sir Ransom?' – and Mrs Spruce cautious and laconic – 'They are his godchildren . . . And descendants of his own failed. The reason sufficed' (241). When Jennet turns up, Bartle asks if she 'brings . . . more scandal'; he is rebuked by Mrs Spruce, and the messenger formally admits, 'Well, I do come, armed with gossip. I confess it was that that brought me. We ought to be above scandal-mongering, but what we ought to be, is not what we are' (242–3). Jennet's message more than satisfies Alice's curiosity: she tells them Sir Ransom was Bridget's father, and about the photographs of a woman with a child and Sir Ransom with the same child and the two revealing letters. This final gossip scene has everything – a fair, reliable, intelligent eavesdropper and avid listeners, including one who tells nothing and knows everything. Mrs Spruce endures hearing her own story crudely related and judged, with the bad news that someone (Gaunt) thought the woman's face looked familiar, and the good news that someone (Selina) burnt the photographs.

Piecemeal telling and listening make listeners and reader wait. The responses of the gossips range from grave reproach to harsh, sanctimonious condemnation and they are all conventional and ignorant. As Mrs Spruce listens, her stress and sorrow are evident: she speaks without looking up and is silent when it seems to be her turn to speak, but she never falters, never lies, never placates public opinion, never says too much. There are dangerous corners: someone mentions the provision known to have been made for her long ago, but the moment passes; she speaks from personal knowledge of Sir Ransom, and Ambrose is surprised but does not dwell on it. She controls herself till Jennet's departure gives her an excuse to leave. She meets Selina in the hall; they exchange looks, and as she goes upstairs to her own room, there is the first physical sign of her ordeal and shock:

> Mrs Spruce pushed back her hair to bring her hand across her face, and went upstairs with a flush spreading over it. She sat down on her bed to grasp and confront her knowledge. She had faced other things in her life, and hardly shrunk from the effort. Then she went to a chest and took out a photograph, and stood with her eyes upon it. It was a copy of the one of a girl with a child, that Gaunt had found, and his mother had destroyed. She held it by her face before the glass, tracing the changes of the years. Then she restored it to its place, and went downstairs, with an air at once resigned and resolute. (254)

It is very likely that we have guessed her secret, because there are many clues: her affection for Bridget and the children, that settlement made long ago, the condolences she sends to Selina after Sir Ransom's death, and her responses during the gossip scenes, including her only tears – when Fanshawe talks about the rumoured incest. But we are likely to read the gossip scene again after we follow Mrs Spruce into her room, and she takes out her copy of the photograph of herself and her child. Another past detail we may remember, and perhaps re-read, is the image of her fifty-nine-year-old face, 'a full, florid face, blue, experienced eyes, a round, full chin that melted into a pillar-like neck, and a curved, red mouth' (62). The description ended suggestively: 'She looked like a girl of twenty, who had lived another thirty-nine years. But this is not what she was' (62). Here – and I think also in the mirror scene – there is a sensuous impact, even an erotic one, though the woman's contemplation of her past attraction in the old photograph is a wry, sad memory of fleshly pleasures. Another strikingly different response to her face is Gaunt's, as he half-thinks he recognises it – 'Not that it was the face of anyone who mattered' – and says those class-callous words 'Not an educated face' (226), which I have quoted.

As I have said, Compton-Burnett rarely shows deep romantic and erotic love, and if the mirror scene may be read as an exception, such a feeling is not the whole or even the most important aspect of its power. It is one of the rare episodes which invites sympathy, by omission and understatement; Mrs Spruce is a sympathetic character but we are not explicitly and excitedly invited to admire or pity her, as we are with Fanny Price, Maggie Tulliver and Dorothea. The mirror scene is charged with almost unstated feeling, and we have to follow its brief, simple narrative slowly and closely, perhaps re-reading, to take it all in. It is a masterpiece of suggestion.

The first sentence describes the woman's involuntary physical response to what she has just heard, not felt until she is alone. The second briefly records the need to 'grasp', before facing, the experience of hearing her own story, superficially re-told and conventionally judged by strangers, brought up to date with the news of her old lover's death. The third is a curt, condensed and elliptical retrospect of character and event, marked by that significant 'hardly' in 'hardly shrunk from the effort'. The fifth images the life-story as she deliberately stages and scans it, as we see her deciding to put together, face, then facing the faces of her youth and her middle age reflected in the glass, the young one in the photograph, the older one in her reflection. The last sentence, which shows feeling as well as describing it, marks a wry but not tragic or ironic acceptance of things as they are: love, age, death, past and future. We feel her feel and accept the weight of experience, by herself. Her self-images are strangely remote: what was and is warm flesh is seen, not touched, in cold inhuman surfaces of glass and paper, further refracted in a novel, written then printed for a reader.

There is no mention of feeling until that last sentence but the brief scene, on the novel's last page, is one of expressive action, described and implied. Compton-Burnett often omits directions for movement, but this reserved narrative is packed with them: the woman sits still, gets up, opens the chest, gets the photograph, stands still, looks at it, holds it to the mirror and looks again. Her stillness suggests intensity and concentration, her business registers eagerness and agitation. There is an austere wit in the play on literal and metaphorical senses of face, the awareness of language, but it is not detached: this is a rare scene where we may admire and sympathise. It is not free-standing: before it, we have seen Mrs Spruce reduced to the status of listener, making reticent but honest comments, and perhaps retraced her understated progress throughout the novel. It is like the episode in *The Arabian Nights* where a life-time goes by in the moment it takes a man to dip his head in water.

The novel's last lines are a brief exchange between servant and mistress, the grandmothers of Rose and Viola. Selina says, 'Miss Chace and Miss Anne will spend the day with us tomorrow. You will do your best for us, as you always have and always will?'; Mrs Spruce says, 'I will,' and she goes 'to the kitchen, knowing what really had passed' (254). This final conversation is in danger of sounding complacent, but it is a dialogue which affirms the past and the future, its harmony truthfully qualified as well as generated by the loneliness of that looking-glass.

Although other characters – Sir Ransom, Mildred, Bridget, Edmund and the less prominent Selina, Gaunt, Emma and Anne Chace – are characters of whom and in whom there is more than meets the eye, they are presented externally and simply, compared with Mrs Spruce. And they lack her ordinary heroic stability. So I believe her story is – in every sense – the heart of the novel, in spite of her neglect by Burkhart, who finds the novel's conclusion negative, mentioning Mrs Spruce in one sentence, simply calling her 'robust', and taking the heroine to be Bridget, whom he judges not sufficiently strong or interesting for that position.[4]

The Chase story is uneventful until Sir Ransom dies, while the stories of Mrs Spruce, Bridget and Mildred are always on the move. Sir Ransom is handsome, sensual, charming, kind and humorous, his qualities shown mostly in ironic conversations about death, and only after death is he seen as having actively determined action and plot. Unlike Mrs Spruce, he is never shown reflecting on the past, and the life and death of his unnamed wife are narrated in three sentences, but his talk with his best friend, Gaunt, and the bequests in his will register his control and satisfaction, within the limits which his class complacency and his reason accept. He jokes about never having done a day's work, but he has provided for Mrs Spruce and taken care of their child, whom he has loved as guardian and god-parent, and whom he would have adopted if his elder daughter had not been unwilling. He has done what he wanted – made sure his inheritance will pass to those of his own blood, preserving the long ancestral line he values, but also provided for whose he loves; when his will is read we understand his irony, enigmatic complacency and reserve when Gaunt was curious about his bequests and anticipated the family being 'wiped out' (25). His fault has paid off, he has apparently not suffered, and of course, unlike the mother of his only fertile child, he has the power of his gender and class. He is given a happy ending, after a fairly happy life. Mrs Spruce's attachment to him importantly and subtly qualifies the class stereotype of squire as seducer. He is also sympathetic as a mortal man approaching death.

That remarkably long and packed seventh chapter, which ends with Mrs Spruce, starts by involving Sir Ransom in the key imagery. His daughter Emma says, 'my father is in the clouds today,' and when Mildred asks, 'A penny for your thoughts,' he 'answered as if he did not know who spoke', says he was wishing he had adopted Bridget when she was a child, and asks Mildred if she seems different after hearing that the incest rumour was false – 'I may ask the question this once' – to be told that she has come out of 'a kind of dusk' into 'a sort of radiance' (199). It is a good moment for Mildred as messenger, and a vibrant response to the title.

Bridget appears with the other Lovats for what is to be her father's last public meal. It is a solemn and comic tea-party, where, at the start, Sir Ransom is in full command of himself and the situation, welcoming Bridget with a resonant 'My dear!', hearing Emma's words for the woman she does not know is her half-sister, 'She must feel a great light over her world,' and Bridget's eloquent and wise, 'it begins to seem the simple light of day. We shall soon be dwelling on the undeserved darkness' (203).

The scene soon darkens, but not in a way expected by characters or readers. First, Mildred, excluded as guest so officious as housekeeper, introduces an abrupt change of key: 'Now, you chattering people, make way for the tea' (203). It is another significant meal. Sir Ransom has what he wants, and can preside as delighted, ironic and witty host, tactful and sensitive when Mildred breaks a valuable Dresden cup, saving her face with his jokes, 'Why, it is behaving like any ordinary cup' and 'A cup is only a cup' (206). His story is about seduction, but also about father-love, and, like Hetty looking at Henry in *A God and His Gifts*, he looks at Bridget with what Emma sees as the expression he wears 'for no one else' and with diplomatic care and sincerity explains 'It may be, my dear. I was thinking of no one else' (204). His composure and elation do not last.

When Mildred is out of the room, Gaunt suggests that she should leave the Chace household, because of the new, embarrassing knowledge that she is Edmund's child; Bridget protests, but when Sir Ransom joins the discussion it is to falter. It is a dramatic failure of life and language: 'It is Gaunt who should go away . . . It is Gaunt who does not forget. But I do not think he will leave me, when I am too old for my friends to go. Gaunt has been my friend.' Gaunt says his voice seems to come 'from a mile away', and the next words come 'from even further': 'We have no time to forget. We have no time for much. We have to begin at the beginning. It is strange that we learn as much as we do. We were born to do very little' (208). He is not to die just yet, but these sets of short, staccato sentences compose his lyrical moment, a fine near-to-death-bed speech which makes life and language strange.

He is the king-pin of the novel, his story told briefly but sufficiently, one minute seated next to the daughter who is his best beloved, then close to death, disclosing 'the place of his will', lying in 'as composed and natural a state as if his eyes were on the future . . . This is actually where they were. It gave him his peace with himself' (208). A less austere novelist might have made him think of the mother of his child, but not this one. But when we come to her great scene, it is also to find composure.

His story goes on after his death, to his will, which announces an unexpected legacy of a third of his estate to his god-daughters and descendants, Bridget and her children, shared with his childless spinster daughters. And a little later, it is discovered from the photographs and letters he never destroyed that he was Bridget's father and her mother was probably an unmarried working-class woman.

In this scene, Mildred Hallam is prominent as well as Sir Ransom, as she moves in and out of the tea-party, in and out of our attention. Like Mrs Spruce, she is a working woman, one of many companion–house-keepers, downtrodden or abused like Miss Griffin in *A Family and a Fortune* and Miss Bunyan in *Daughters and Sons*; independent, like Miss Lacy in *Elders and Betters* and Edith Hallam in *Daughters and Sons*. In the first chapter, we saw Mildred as the housekeeper who was needed when Lady Chace died and her daughters were unwilling to work, then later as governess to Rose and Viola, starting before she knows and we know they are her half-sisters. In the last chapter, we know she is closely related to the guests at the table from which she is excluded, why courteous Sir Ransom demurs at her exclusion, why he is too absorbed to make more fuss, why she is intrusive and why she breaks the cup. She is a more complex version of bossy, competent and unsexy women like Justine in *Men and Wives*, Luce in *Parents and Children* and the harshly simplified Dulcia in *A House and Its Head*. She is an unattractive character but we probably feel guilty about finding her unattractive. Self-satisfied, over-confident and conventional, but honest, kind and intelligent, she is 'no dullard', as she tells Gaunt when he is patronisingly surprised by her comment that potatoes are more necessary than peaches but we all like a peach. Her pupils' verdict that she expects too much feeling is shrewd; she is often pathetic and unsympathetic, especially in her own patronising ways, but, though charmless and less brainy than her half-sisters, she is perceptive about Rose's 'brain', which 'gives rise to charm', and Viola's 'charm', which 'depends on brain' (200). She is less protected and sheltered than Justine, Luce and Dulcia; she knows when to get out; she is sensible about accepting affection and money from her father and grandmother. When she overhears the conversation about the will, sees the photograph of a 'nurse' or 'some farm-girl who looked after the child', and hears Gaunt's words, 'no-one who mattered' and 'not a person in the story', she thinks of studying 'the waiting-women in fiction' (227). The touch of creativity and meta-narrative draws us to Mrs Spruce, the waiting-woman who does matter and who is a person in the story, but also emphasises Mildred's own un-self-pitying position as a waiting-woman, while leaving open the question of her self-awareness. She occupies an important social space between the upper-class women in the Chace and Lovat houses, and Mrs Spruce.

The story of Bridget and Edmund Lovat is more conspicuous than any of the others, more lengthily, explicitly and emotionally told, and emphasised by the recurrent imagery that makes *Darkness and Day* stand out from the other novels, and which is more concentrated in their part of the story. The title is first reflected by the sunshine and rain of real weather, then images Bridget's and Edmund's distress and secret, as they keep dark their belief that their marriage is incestuous, feeling horror, guilt, shame and sexual inhibition, which deepen as the story spreads, as real darkness does, and spread to other people living less clouded lives. The children's imagination contributes: Viola is not afraid of 'the dark' but of 'pieces of light and darkness' (87), and says 'the shadows are coming upstairs, and they will go on until it is light. And Rose doesn't see them, and so she can't protect me' (104). They are Viola's shadows but next day Rose hides behind a sofa, rising from the floor to be seen as 'a shadow' vanishing upstairs (118). As we have seen, Mildred describes Bridget's 'radiance' after the incest story is disproved, and Bridget welcomes 'the simple light of day' (199; 203). Characters reflect on their own use of image, as when Edmund develops and renews a recurring metaphor – 'The cloud must be lighter as it spreads . . .

But it must spread no further' – which the more introspective Bridget analyses and discards – 'A cloud is the word we use. It seems a strange one. The trouble is at the base of our lives, at the root of the children's being' (113).

The articulate servants take part in the subtle, playful analysis of language, and the imagery recurs: an unspecified speaker who is almost certainly Mrs Spruce asks, 'Bartle, are you blind to the light and shade in everyday life?' (99), and 'cloud' and 'clouded' return as dead and mixed metaphors when Bartle gloats, 'This is the cloud and the mystery that hangs over people' (141), and Fanshawe, the nurse, apologises, 'I am sorry a cloud has been cast, and that I was the unwilling instrument' (145).

The reserved narrator and the characters make pictures which urge us to ask questions. The day that clears the first darkness begins to darken again, as days do, but is the day all that bright and the darkness all that dark? The dark and the day are outside us and inside, and the relation between the two, causal and rhetorical, is not always clear. Dead metaphors revive and die again. There are many darknesses and lights, clouds and shadows, and the cycle only comes to a stop with the last page of the novel, where the title still applies: everyone is in the dark, except the two wise women left in creative complicity. A vibrant ending brings enlightenment, relationship and resolution to them, but their day depends on darkness.

The novel is poetic in prose style as well as in its imagery. Robert Liddell printed two speeches by Bridget and Edmund from this novel as verse, at the same time drawing attention to a resemblance to the poetic drama of T. S. Eliot: 'A tendency to verse, perhaps not altogether intended, perhaps given more attention than it should be by an ear accustomed to some of Mr Eliot's later rhythms, seems to mark some of the later books.'[5] The early poems and *The Waste Land* may have left an impression on her style, but the 'later rhythms' of Eliot's verse drama, and the Greek drawing-room plays which are most like her books, came after Compton-Burnett began writing her post-war novels, so the South Kensington neighbours may have influenced each other.

The play closest to Compton-Burnett, and especially to this novel, is *The Family Reunion*, not only in its relation to Greek tragedy but in its subject, and in its shift from a prosaic resolved blank verse, at times moving towards hexameter, to a more measured and formal form and language in certain heightened passages, comparable to the arias of opera. In this story of family reunions, a similar style and occasional shifts in tone and language are almost entirely reserved for Edmund and Bridget, chief carriers of the dominant imagery. When Selina hears that her eldest son and his wife are coming home, she exclaims, 'I cannot avoid the lyric note. I am lifted out of myself' (58), but her self-awareness and metaphor are much less lyrical than the poetry sustained and separated by the couple alienated by what they think is an incestuous marriage. There are times when they speak as if they are, as Bridget says, 'in a play'.

Back after three years' absence, and after briefly greeting his mother and brother, Edmund strikes a formal pose and a grand style.

> Edmund moved aside, as though to address the group.
> 'We are going to have what we should always have had. To be to each other what we might have been. The future is to have its sorrow running through it, its question of the shadow over certain lives, its darkness at the back of the day. We will not try to forget it; that carries the danger of remembrance. But we can try to turn our eyes from it, and keep them to the light.'
> 'What are we to read into that?' said Gaunt.
> 'Read nothing into it, until you can read the truth. Tomorrow will bring it to you. I am dealing in mysteries, clouding our first hour. But we will make no promise we cannot fulfil. We do not choose what we give.' (80)

The family's response is also formally described:

> The threat in Edmund's words, his alien note, the presence and silence of his wife laid a spell on his hearers and held their speech. This atmosphere came from the past. There had to be a pause before the present could receive it.

Grant is responsive to the 'alien note' when he says there seems to be 'something ominous over us', and Edmund resumes it: 'There is nothing there has not always been. But it is to be seen as what it is, and that will not leave it the same. A hard and strange moment is before us' (80–1).

That brief narrative phrase, 'his alien note', draws attention to tone and feeling as characters step outside themselves, with self-characterisations like those in Elizabethan drama, which may also act as a formal prelude or overture. These self-commentaries echo the key words of the title, before we modulate to a line of ordinary speech and the children's voices outside. In their bedroom that night, Bridget and Edmund discuss the secret they are going to divulge; she dreads facing her mother-in-law, he tries to reassure her, but what starts as unremarkable domestic and marital discussion gathers force and ends in formal poetic antiphony.

At the heart of the dialogue are two balanced speeches sharing rhetoric and tone: Bridget speaks of the 'blackness' over them which 'blots out the future', uses the image of tragedy – 'I know I am using tragic words but they are words' – and asks, 'What light words are there to use?' He replies, 'We cannot use light words, but we could use none. But you have overborne me … You will say what you must, shed your own light, bring your own darkness,' and there follows one of the speeches[6] Liddell lineated as verse:

'We are fluent, Edmund. We have said it before. We seem to be acting a scene. And that is what we are doing. But it will not help us when the time comes. The scene will rise out of the moment, as scenes do. I can feel your mother's eyes on me, my own eyes falling before them. These rehearsals will not stand us in any stead.'

'Yes, that is the sadness in our sorrow, that it takes the guise of shame. That is what I would spare you, if you would be spared. Shame is no less, that it is helpless, and pity may carry much that destroys itself. And we shall face it in its hardest form, the form that carries self-pity. We shall have to give pity ourselves.' (109)

We go back to conversational dialogue, Bridget reverting to 'her other tone' (109) after the formality of the dialogue which was so lyrically repetitive, regularly rhythmical, alliterative and imagistic. The novel's dominant images are the darkness and day of the title and also the imagery of tragedy and drama. The lyricism depersonalises language and characters, as do the stage directions and the discussion of language; the impersonal narrator and the two characters speak with an awareness of themselves, the words they use, the actions outside the self, and the images of their title, as if they know they are characters in fiction, in this fiction, the title their predestination, as of course it is. They speak of the theatrical genre and the tragic genre as if they know they are characters in a play, and a tragedy. The common theatrical terms like 'scene', 'rehearsal', 'tragic' and 'tragedy' here become more generic, thematic and portentous, less wit than poetry. The self-consciousness of Bridget and Edmund is tragic, since what they deludedly feel to be their darkness threatens to destroy their identity as husband and wife, brother and sister, mother and father. There is estrangement in more senses than one, as all the family relationships are destabilised and confused by what is felt as the tragedy of incest.

Next day, the Lovat family gathers for the promised revelation: Bridget cannot face the telling but Edmund does, and there once again is a shift from matter-of-fact, ordinary tones and diction to tragic poetry. Edmund starts in the plain, relaxed style, briefly recounting his love affair, his illegitimate child, his marriage to Bridget, and her identification as his daughter. Bridget finds the scene easier than she expected, but her speech about feeling relaxed becomes intense, formally repetitive and imagistic, and Edmund joins her thinking and shares her poetry:

'The load is off my heart, though its reason remains. It may return; I suppose it must; but there is the moment of peace.'
'The cloud must be lighter as it spreads,' said Edmund. 'But it must spread no further.'
'A cloud is the word we use. It seems a strange one.' (113)

After a little more in the formal solemn style, Edmund hopes his mother and brother will not suffer, his mother says they must suffer with them, and there is a shift to a lighter vein with Bridget's dry and even amused, 'We need not be afraid it has fallen flat,' a line described as 'in her other tone' (113), the phrase also used in the rehearsal scene the previous evening (109). Like the 'alien note' heard by Gaunt on the first evening, such stage direction points up the shifts in linguistic register, the detached meta-language which makes language strange and increases emotional intensity. It invokes the power of the past, that 'something ominous' which Gaunt felt overpowering the sense of individual identity (81). Now he takes his brief turn centre-stage as, horrified and thrilled, he insists that this is tragedy:

'I will follow the matter to its end. If Edmund's daughters marry, their children will not only be their grandchildren. And Bridget will not only be their grandmother. Bridget has done and suffered the traditional tragic things. As nearly the same as Oedipus, as a woman could.' (117)

It is compulsive repetition, a kind of chant listing the horrors – but perhaps exorcising them.

Because they are not facts – it was not incest, after all, only imagined incest – but we cannot really say 'after all', because the imagination brought suffering, estrangement, and a lost sense of identity and relationship. Still, it is not tragedy, as is made very clear, aptly enough, through comedy. This move of genre is made, and made explicit, by Selina, the wise humourist who jokes about Oedipus. Gaunt insists, 'tragic things . . . nearly the same as Oedipus . . . the difference is, as she said herself, that she has not put out her eyes' (117), but Selina has her moment when she observes,

'Perhaps we are fortunate ... Or perhaps fashions have changed. It does not seem that Oedipus was thought to have acted oddly under the circumstances. Or to have been exacting in requiring his daughters' attendance for the rest of his days.'

And 'He went about from town to town, talking about it. But I don't think Bridget would do that' (117). It is serious joking and Selina earns her final prominence when she burns the incriminating photograph and finds the right words to communicate with Mrs Spruce. Selina gains in stature but Mrs Spruce is given the very last words, as is right.

After the appropriate formality and lyricism in this part of the novel, and the challenge in the understandable use of the words tragic and tragedy, the rejection of tragedy becomes clear. It may be made sufficiently implicit for the reader alert to cues of the meta-narrative, but the demystifying shift from poetic intensities to the prosaic comic commentary makes sure no one misses the point. The novel dismisses the very concept and genre of tragedy for a post-Darwinian world – which was also post-Sophoclean and post-Aeschylean. The novelist studied Greek tragedy thoroughly and deeply enough to understand the genre, and found it no longer available to a modern rationalist who had no gods to question.

The rotating actions move in contrast and parallel, constructed to support and explain each other, in changing roles, taking their turn to dominate the action. We see Sir Ransom, Bridget, Edmund, Mildred and others, as they fall or rise, succeed or suffer, thanks or no thanks to birth, class, gender, money and luck, and we see Mrs Spruce survive with courage and integrity. No one and no action in the novel is tragic, but no one and nothing is satirically reduced or instrumentalised either. Selina comically dismisses tragedy but moves away from her ironic style, Sir Ransom reveals himself affectively right to his end, and Mrs Spruce seriously engrosses the last chapter to dominate the novel, in retrospect.

Notes

1. Henry James, *The Art of the Novel*, 84. 'What do such large baggy monsters, with their queer elements of the accidental and the arbitrary, artistically mean?'

2. Margaret Jourdain and Ivy Compton-Burnett, 'A Conversation between I. Compton-Burnett and Margaret Jourdain', in *The Art of I. Compton-Burnett*, ed. Burkhart, 1; 24.
3. Michael Millgate, 'Interview with Miss Compton-Burnett', in *The Art of Ivy Compton-Burnett*, ed. Burkhart, 11; 39.
4. Charles Burkhart, *I. Compton-Burnett*, 120–1.
5. Robert Liddell, *The Novels of I. Compton-Burnett*, 110. Liddell re-lineates as verse:

> 'We are fluent, Edmund. We have said it before.
> We seem to be acting a scene. And that is what we are doing.
> But it will not help us when the time comes.
> The scene will rise out of the moment, as scenes do.
> I can feel your mother's eyes on me, my own eyes falling before them.
> These rehearsals will not stand us in any stead.' (111)

6. The other is a speech of Sir Roderic Shelley's (like Sir Ransom, a man with a secret past) in *Two Worlds and Their Ways*: 'It is the hidden thing that does not flourish . . . Nothing can grow without the light. We can only tend it as we can, leaving it safe in the dark. And although "out of sight" may not mean "out of mind", this talk must be as if it had not been' (240). There are echoes of Eliot's *Family Reunion* (1939) in the words, rhythm and image of darkness.

Bibliography

Novels by Ivy Compton-Burnett

Brothers and Sisters (London: Allison & Busby, 1929).
Darkness and Day (London: Gollancz, 1951).
Daughters and Sons (London: Gollancz, 1937).
Dolores (Edinburgh: Blackwood, 1911).
Dolores (Edinburgh: Blackwood, 1971).
Elders and Betters (London: Gollancz, 1944).
A Family and a Fortune (London: Gollancz, 1939).
A Father and His Fate (London: Gollancz, 1957).
A God and His Gifts (London: Gollancz, 1963).
A Heritage and Its History (London: Gollancz, 1959).
A House and Its Head (London: Heinemann, 1935).
The Last and the First (London, British Library, MS 57851 A-L: 1964–1969).
The Last and the First (London: Gollancz, 1971).
Manservant and Maidservant (London: Gollancz, 1947).
Men and Wives (London: Heinemann, 1931).
The Mighty and Their Fall (London: Gollancz, 1961).
More Women than Men (London: Heinemann, 1933).
Mother and Son (London: Gollancz, 1955).
The Novels of I. Compton-Burnett: Limited Edition, 19 vols (London: Gollancz, 1972).
Parents and Children (London: Gollancz, 1941).
Pastors and Masters: A Study (London: Heath Cranton, 1925).
The Present and the Past (London: Gollancz, 1953).
Two Worlds and Their Ways (London: Gollancz, 1949).

Interviews by Ivy Compton-Burnett

Dick, Kay, *Ivy and Stevie: Ivy Compton-Burnett and Stevie Smith: Conversations and Reflections* (London: Duckworth, 1971).

Jourdain, Margaret and Ivy Compton-Burnett, 'A Conversation between I. Compton-Burnett and Margaret Jourdain', *Orion*, 1 (1945), pp. 20–8 (repr. in Charles Burkhart (ed.), *The Art of I. Compton-Burnett* (London: Gollancz, 1972), pp. 21–31).

Millgate, Michael, 'Interview with Miss Compton-Burnett', *Review of English Literature*, 3 (1962), pp. 96–112 (repr. in Charles Burkhart (ed.), *The Art of I. Compton-Burnett* (London: Gollancz, 1972), pp. 32–47).

Other books and articles

Austen, Jane [1814], *Mansfield Park* (Oxford: Oxford University Press, 2003).

Austen, Jane [1818], *Northanger Abbey* (London: Penguin, 2003).

Baldanza, Frank, *Ivy Compton-Burnett* (New York: Twayne Publishers, [1964]).

Bowen, Elizabeth, 'Elders and Betters', in *The Art of I. Compton-Burnett: A Collection of Critical Essays* (London: Gollancz, 1972), pp. 58–63.

Bruner, Jerome S., Alison Jolly and Kathy Sylva (eds), *Play: Its Role in Development and Evolution* (Harmondsworth: Penguin, 1976).

Burkhart, Charles (ed.), *The Art of I. Compton-Burnett: A Collection of Critical Essays* (London: Gollancz, 1972).

Burkhart, Charles, *I. Compton-Burnett* (London: Gollancz, 1965).

Butler, Samuel, *Samuel Butler's Notebooks*, ed. Geoffrey Keynes and Brian Hill (London: Jonathan Cape, 1951).

Carroll, Robert and Stephen Prickett (eds), *The Bible: Authorized King James Version* (Oxford: Oxford University Press, 2008).

Coleridge, Samuel Taylor [1817], *Biographia Literaria* (London: J. M. Dent & Sons, 1956).

Coleridge, Samuel Taylor, *Shakespearean Criticism*, ed. T. M. Raysor (London: J. M. Dent & Sons, 1960).

Douglas, Mary, *Implicit Meanings*, 2nd edn (London: Routledge, 1999).

Eliot, George [1871–2], *Middlemarch* (London: Penguin, 1994).

Frischknecht, Ruth, 'Ivy Compton-Burnett: Kritische Betrachtung ihrer Werke', *Sammlung schweizerischer Dissertationen. Reihe der Philosophie I* (Winterthur: Schellenberg, 1961).

Gentile, Kathy Justice, *Ivy Compton-Burnett* (London: Macmillan Education, 1991).

Graham, Loretta Beth Kemper, *Finding Her Place: Ivy Compton-Burnett as a Country-House Novelist* (Lexington: University of Kentucky, 2004).

Grieg, Cicely, *Ivy Compton-Burnett: A Memoir* (London: Garnstone Press, 1972).

Groos, Karl, *The Play of Man*, trans. E. L. Baldwin (London: Heinemann, 1901).

Hardy, Barbara, *The Exposure of Luxury: Radical Themes in Thackeray* (London: Peter Owen, 1972).

Hardy, Barbara, 'Lying, Cruelty, Secrecy and Alienation in I. Compton-Burnett's *Elders and Betters*', in Rod Mengham and N. H. Reeve (eds), *The Fiction of the 1940s* (Palgrave: Basingstoke, 2001), pp. 134–51.

Hardy, Barbara, '*Middlemarch*: Public and Private Worlds', in *Particularities: Readings in George Eliot* (Peter Owen: London, 1982), pp. 104–25.

Hardy, Barbara, *The Moral Art of Dickens* (London: Athlone, 1970).

Hardy, Barbara, *Tellers and Listeners: The Narrative Imagination* (London: Athlone, 1975).

Huizinga, Johan [1938], *Homo Ludens: A Study of the Play Element in Human Culture* (London: Paladin, 1970).

James, Henry [1909], *The Art of the Novel* (London: Charles Scribner's Sons, 1947).

James, Henry, *The Critical Muse: Selected Literary Criticism* (Harmondsworth: Penguin, 1987).

Kant, Immanuel [1790], *Critique of Judgement*, trans. James Creed Meredith, rev. Nicholas Walker (Oxford: Oxford University Press, 2007).

Lawrence, D. H., *Phoenix: The Posthumous Papers of D. H. Lawrence* (London: Heinemann, 1936).

Liddell, Robert, *The Novels of I. Compton-Burnett* (London: Gollancz, 1955).

Light, Alison, *Forever England: Femininity, Literature and Conservatism Between the Wars* (London: Routledge, 1991).

Mauss, Marcel, *The Gift*, trans. Ian Cunnison (London: Cohen & West, 1966).

Mennell, Stephen, Anne Murcott and Anneke H. van Otterloo, *The Sociology of Food: Eating, Diet and Culture* (London: Sage, 1992).

Nevius, Blake, *Ivy Compton-Burnett* (London: Columbia University Press, 1970).

Ortega y Gasset, José, *The Dehumanization of Art and Other Essays on Art, Culture, and Literature* (Princeton: Princeton University Press, 1968).

Piaget, J., *Play, Dreams and Imitation in Childhood* (London: Routledge & Kegan Paul, 1951).

Plato, *The Republic*, 2nd edn, trans. H. D. P. Lee (London: Penguin, 2007).

Powell, Violet, *A Compton-Burnett Compendium* (London: Heinemann, 1973).

Sackville-West, Edward, 'Ladies Whose Bright Pens', in Charles Burkhart (ed.), *The Art of I. Compton-Burnett* (London: Gollancz, 1972), pp. 103–22.

Shklovsky, Viktor [1916], 'Art as Technique', in Julie Rivkin and Michael Ryan (eds), *Literary Theory: An Anthology* (Malden, MA: Blackwell, 2004), pp. 15–21.

Smith, Patricia Juliana, *Lesbian Panic: Homoeroticism in Modern British Women's Fiction* (New York: Columbia University Press, 1997).

Sprigge, Elizabeth, *The Life of Ivy Compton-Burnett* (London: Gollancz, 1973).

Spurling, Hilary, *Ivy When Young: The Early Life of I. Compton-Burnett, 1884–1919* (London: Gollancz, 1974).

Spurling, Hilary, *Secrets of a Woman's Heart* (Harmondsworth: Penguin, 1985).

Sturgeon, Theodore, *More Than Human* (London: Gollancz, 1954).

Virgil, *The Aeneid*, trans. C. Day Lewis (London: Hogarth Press, 1952).

Wyndham, John, *The Midwich Cuckoos* (Harmondsworth: Penguin, 1969).

Index